MASTER BUCK

I0413865

Andrew R. Bennett

Master Buck

by Andrew R. Bennett

Photo Credits:

Front Cover photo and interior image from 123RF.com
Back cover photo by Beverly Bennett

Copyright ©2017 by Andrew R. Bennett

ISBN 978-1543238419

Printed in the United States of America

PRGott Books Publishing
Norway, Maine
www.prgottbooks.net

For Perry and Uncle Dan M.,

the best hunters I ever went down a mountain with

–CHAPTER 1–

The first night Sejanus traveled over five miles. Known territory, safe places, ground that he had grown up on and had provided him succor now only infuriated him. Abandoning all caution, he tore at sturdy trees and ripped the earth with displeasure and fear.

Fighting himself, he rested the next morning in a thicket of dense, dark fir with the wind and a quiet river at his back. In the middle of that sunny afternoon he finally slept and woke up hungry, but he would not eat until after dark.

The next night he went eight miles in a straight line. He was now at the edge of his home territory. As the evening stars shifted over him toward the pale beginning of a frigid dawn, he found a hemlock knoll with three avenues of escape which overlooked a small brook that he knew would guide him to his next destination. Sejanus sensed the danger that he was in, but strange urges had erupted in him and the only way to deal with those urges was to go on one more evening beyond his home range. Perhaps at that time some of the vexing questions which had been plaguing him would be answered to some degree.

Sejanus was an extraordinary animal by any standard. He was taller and much longer than other mature bucks. His body was so huge that a couple of times his life had been spared because hunters had witnessed his passing during low light in heavy cover and had not dared to shoot because, as one ruefully stated later, "I thought it was a damned moose!"

It was surprising that that hunter had not spied Sejanus' antlers because, as huge as his body was, his antlers nevertheless were disproportionally large for his body. Unlike many of the bucks in that region, the antlers of Sejanus did not come forward over his head in the typical "swamp deer" fashion. The rack of Sejanus was of the "open woods" style with the beams extending well beyond his ears in a handsome manner. Though the inside spread of his horns was a bit over twenty-eight inches and nearly seven inches in circumference at their base and therefore easily seen when in the open,

Sejanus nevertheless had no problem whatsoever in keeping them hidden from view when he felt that he was being hunted by man.

For the first five years of his life Sejanus had been more or less a normal buck, breeding every doe he could in order to produce as many offspring as possible. Using his intimate knowledge of his home range, he had easily avoided those who would kill him if they could. Hunters marveled at the girth of his track and at the size of the trees that he rubbed, but they saw him not. Coydogs knew better then to expend valuable energy pursuing a creature that could effortlessly leap thirty feet with a single bound. Besides, this one had the nasty habit of entering very close cover and had antlers which could shred small trees on the way to their hearts.

No, Sejanus knew how to be left alone and could have been satisfied with that as most bucks were. But he wasn't. Late in the summer of his fifth year something tipped the axis of what made him tick. Breeding every available doe in his home territory had not yielded the results he wanted, the results he needed. Somewhere down beyond the end of that rather mundane looking brook below him was the answer to the current urges which would end up dominating the rest of his life.

Yes, he was now a line buck. With a single-minded purpose and unyielding determination, Sejanus would attempt to secure a spot on a very slippery stage. He had roughly another eight miles to go now. She was there. But so, also, was the beginning of the territory of Essene.

–CHAPTER 2–

In the late fall Essene lived in a world of silver circles. From his core area located in the beginning of a large swamp, the sun seemed to neither rise nor set. Where he lay he had two brooks, one large and one small, both deep, protecting at least half of what he surveyed at all times. Looking out, dense groves of small white maple would curl the incoming light through young fir and into cones of silvery light which could be read as accurately as any detection system set up by man.

This nondescript point in the swamp, which had only a slight rise in elevation to it, had three distinct and secure paths of escape. Within each of those three paths, using cover and dips in the land, he had three or four other options to choose from to evade potential harm, if necessary. Sometimes, with great expertise and patience, sometimes he would use them all when the numbers poised against him required it.

Dense, nearly solid walls of small fir and young hemlock guarded his back, assisted by prevailing winds from the north and northwest. Within those nearly impassable stands his escape routes weaved, first in small circles and then in larger ones as danger escalated and dictated his options.

Two subdued, barely detectable points of land pointed directly toward his hiding place. Though everything in back of him looked flat, it wasn't. These two points of land, one coming from a northeasterly direction and the other from the east, created three very shallow gullies which were well hidden by the liberal amount of softwood stands about. Essene had only to slip down over into one of these depressions (for that's all these gullies were), stay motionless or lay down, and usually he was safe.

However, what really contributed the most to his inner sanctum's security was its overpowering anonymity. Where the two subdued points of land came reluctantly and confusedly together was a large flat which rose slightly above the floor of the swamp. This flat was populated by a significant stand of mostly large white pine. It was open here and easy walking for any creature which ventured through it, hunter and hunted alike. All the deer hid in the swamp when they were under duress, but they all had their individual, favorite spots there, and none of them pointed to his area. His stretch of swamp looked like all the rest of it, unbroken, monolithic, and impossible to decipher for the most part.

The most important factor contributing to this state of almost perfect anonymity was the presence of food. The white pine stand was somewhat under a quarter of a mile in width. On the far side of the stand, away from the swamp, was a sprinkling of good-sized oak and beech trees. These oak and beech trees were the dominant trees here. There was plenty of water and sun and good soil drainage to encourage their presence.

On good years, when the mast crop was plentiful, life was easy for Essene. When he returned from his nighttime ramblings during the rut, he would smell for danger, edge along through these hardwoods, eat his fill, and then head to his lair in the swamp. There he would rest, dream of his successes the night before, and then head back out for more fun and fighting as soon as it was pitch black once more.

Because of his enormous size, he didn't have to do a lot of fighting. Unlike Sejanus, Essene wasn't abnormally long but he was abnormally wide with a low center of gravity. After many generations of being bred for the physical limitations of the wetlands, Essene's body appeared to be short. This was so he could maneuver and disappear quickly in the tangled, swampy environment.

His antlers were quite different from those of Sejanus also. In the manner of all true swamp bucks, his massive antlers swept over the front of his face in a massive, bony white fan which he utilized with frightening efficiency when confronting any would be rivals to his throne.

When the rut approached, he would clean the velvet from his horns mostly in his core area to avoid drawing any undue attention to himself. This core area was where he would spend most of his dark period, when his raging hormones would gradually, starting in early autumn, gradually pinch him off from his normal self. During this time his main obsession was to achieve total solitude. This solitude would help to keep him safe from the dangers poised from his many enemies and rivals. The only exception to this condition was to be totally alone with the most dominant doe he could locate as they hid out from all the lesser bucks who would, if they got the chance, pass on their inferior genes if Essene did not persevere over his paranoid tendencies and find his way beyond the natural reticence of these dominant matriarchs.

Essene never came near this place of psychological darkness when the madness of the rut wasn't upon him. However, during the stark, intense days of late autumn, to attract any attention, even of birds and squirrels, was not in his program. For any creature, especially dangerous creatures such as coydogs, to have any inkling of his whereabouts was something he and his mother started working on almost from the very first moment he was up from the frosty, April earth to begin his life. Getting to and from his central core area discreetly during the rut was an obsession which only grew stronger the older he got.

Yes, during the rut Essene was a dangerous neurotic, but for most of the year he was actually a reasonably sociable fellow. Once the rut was over in early winter, he would leave his lair in the swamp and hang out with the other deer in safe areas which could provide food and cover. Not with other deer exactly, but somewhere near them. There was safety in numbers. When they moved, he moved. When they ran, he ran. The deer herd was in a perpetual game of cat and mouse with their only real enemy at this time, the coydogs.

For those who survived the winter, this social situation would sort of carry on into the summer, though not in such a rigid manner. Once the dangers of winter had passed, the whole dynamic relaxed with the easy living of summer.

A mile and a half from where Essene hung out during the rut was a small, isolated field located in the center of a huge block of woods. Along the outside of this block of woods, which was roughly three miles across at its widest part, were four large fields separated by small apple orchards and strips of woods liberally interspersed with heavy brush. A good sized brook managed to touch on the sides of two of these fields. It was deer heaven.

On the far back edge of the centrally located, isolated field was a cozy stand of mature pine where Essene liked to hang his rack during the summer months. Most of the time he would remain close to this region and would only occasionally embark on long, solitary sojourns to the outer perimeters of his territory. These sojourns would usually occur during the later stages of summer when the approach of fall would start to tug at his hormones.

As was common during the summer, all the lesser bucks in the area would gravitate together into a loosely held group. Essene would take the time to find out where they were and camp out near them. He would hang around them but rarely, if ever, with them. Only if actual danger broke out as when, for instance, a pack of voracious coydogs appeared out of the rain and fog, only then would he run alongside these bachelor bucks, adroitly finding ways to crisscross amongst his compatriots through the thickets and swamps before he would expertly curl away to one side and silently allow the coydogs to pass ignorantly by. One might be tempted to say that Essene rather enjoyed the diversion.

So, once in a while the shiftless bachelor bucks served a useful purpose. As a rule however, Essene would remain at a discreet distance from these young rogues. Bachelor bucks were a notoriously rowdy bunch, forever testing each other to see who was stronger or possessed the cleverness and wherewithal to rise up through the pecking order. Essene had no desire to participate in such niceties. The less these other deer knew about him, the better he liked it. If one of the more dominant members of the bachelor group tried to approach him, he would slink off or, if necessary, pin back his ears to display his displeasure at their imprudent rudeness.

Was Essene injured? Lame? Showing signs of wear and tear or otherwise losing his competitive edge? This would be the type of information a lesser buck might be attempting to glean out of him when they made these outrageous approaches upon his presence, and sometimes, even in summer, he might be forced to kick some immature butt.

These bachelor guys, Essene didn't really care that much about, but he had to keep the record straight. If a truly dominant buck were to invade his territory during the rut and see these lesser bucks acting boldly, then he, the invading buck, might get the wrong idea. A showdown might then occur, which, more often than not, would lead to the rapid decline, and even death, of the loser. Essene felt it was much better to keep everyone guessing.

But again, he wasn't entirely anti-social. Immersed as he was in his summer self, free from the raging hormones and paranoia of the rut, he would go on long, leisurely journeys around the surrounding countryside to check up on what his other half had wrought the fall before. After all, what could be more cute or captivating then watching the antics of one of his fawns experiencing its first summer in this world? He would rest and then roam, rest and then roam, until he would witness all the results of his genetic intensity. Rubbing the moss from his newly grown antlers as he went along, he would discreetly, peacefully, seek out his offspring and draw energy from their youthful vitality.

With age had come wisdom. Each year there were less and less does to check up on. Essene had come to know, even during the insanity of the rut, where his presence would count the most. Instinctively, he knew his genes would go forward. Now it was only a question of how far.

On this particular morning, a mile and a half away, along a small river which skirted a narrow, productive hay field, a crow called out with confidence and good cheer. The wind came from that direction. Essene lifted his nose and checked out what it had to offer. There was no danger there. Today he would visit Phyla.

–CHAPTER 3–

Phyla shyly nosed her way into an area of newly grown ferns. Not long ago a cow moose with two calves had barged through here, and Phyla was intent on following their path. Phyla's family had always hung round moose, as much they were allowed to. Some moose didn't mind it and some did. There was no apparent rhyme-nor-reason to it.

Phyla's great-grandfather had started it all when his mother had been slain by hunters during his first year. An old, grey cow moose with a friendly, good natured yearling calf sort of took him in when he persisted in hanging around them, following his mother's death. The moose happened to be of a subservient disposition, while he was a domineering sort of individual.

After losing his mother, this young buck soon became extremely paranoid. It wasn't long before his mild moose benefactors picked up on this trait and were soon acting just as spooky as he was. This development was directly responsible for his long and successful life. The moose, using their wide noses and greater height, picked up on approaching danger just as quickly, if not quicker, than deer could. It wasn't long before they were sneaking quietly through the thickest fir they could find, content to let the young buck sneak along between them, well hidden from the prying eyes of potential predators.

During the time of Phyla's great-grandfather, moose hunting had not been allowed in that zone, and therefore the moose did not perceive themselves as necessarily being in danger when a man came around with a gun. A natural sort of caution might kick in when a human came too close, but on the whole, moose didn't pay that much attention to the shiny-faced intruders who stumbled around them every fall. Future generations of Phyla's great-grandfather's moose benefactors would go from subservient individuals to dominant ones because of what this orphaned buck had taught them.

Soon however, there came the occasional tall tales of skittish moose flitting through the underbrush with all the alacrity of a veteran whitetail. The great-grandfather and his moose family lived in a rough, remote area, so their little secret was a well-kept one for several years. Finally however a substantial, late season snow came and stayed on the ground.

Sensing an opportunity, an experienced hunter decided to do a solitary hunt through a tract of land that he seldom visited. There was a heavy wind that day, and, using it to his advantage, the hunter slowly made his way down a slippery slope that he had been through only a few times in his life.

After a long and careful hunt, he finally saw the telltale movement of deer far down ahead of him in the dark brush. He waited, hoping to get a good look at the animals, but, as is so often the case, the movement soon dwindled and then disappeared altogether. Disappointed, the hunter went to the place where he felt he had seen the movement to determine whether or not the deer merited any further attention.

Once he got around the area in question, at first all he saw were moose tracks which troubled him somewhat. He had hunted his entire life and he knew beyond a shadow of a doubt that the animal he had seen had been a deer. The other movements he had seen might well have been something else, but that initial sighting had definitely been a deer. It took some thorough investigating but finally, not too far below the moose tracks, were the tracks of a huge white-tail buck. The buck was traveling with the moose. He tracked the three for a while but finally all he was following were moose tracks. Darkness was fast approaching in the western foothills. He had no choice but to abandon the search and he never again came across the soon-to-be legendary family again, though over the next few years, he did try from time to time. The moose became very good deer in the end. No snow was ever deep enough after that to give their secret away.

Though in the grand scheme of things, the relationship between Phyla's great-grandfather and the two moose never amounted to too much; the fact of the matter remains that, among the deer family, the mothers teach the young. The two moose that Phyla's great-grandfather had traveled with happened to be cow moose. From that point forward all the descendants of those two moose were, at the very least, not openly hostile to deer in general and to Phyla's family in particular. Phyla, being an intelligent individual, picked up on this.

Though she never developed anywhere near the relationship that her great-grandfather had with the moose, she had nevertheless been taught by her mother not to avoid a certain discreet amount of contact with their larger cousins. This was, by in large, the main reason she had followed the moose into the ferns. The moose up ahead were friends to her family, whether they knew it or not.

An impatient commotion around her rear hocks told Phyla that her single fawn had seen all he needed to of this particular spot. She moved ahead until a subdued reaction from the still invisible moose told her that a sufficient introduction had been made. They now knew of her fawn. They had smelled and had probably seen him. That would be enough for now. She had achieved two things: shown the fawn to the moose, while using the moose to discourage the presence of coydogs. Coydogs didn't fool with cow moose with calves.

The patch of ferns was beside a brook, and the brook was not that far from a field. The mosquitoes had been thick this day, but the scent of the large moose nearby had drawn a lot of them away. There was also a good breeze coming out of the field which told Phyla that there was no danger in that direction and even less mosquitoes. The field had nutritious food that would provide robust milk for her fawn. Phyla tested the air once more. It was safe. She left the cover of the ferns.

–CHAPTER 4–

Essene approached the field through a heavy screen of thick, young hemlock. In the cool green darkness of the hemlock boughs, he observed the patches of the hay field he could readily see as it shimmered in the mid-day heat. Fighting all his instincts, he yielded to the lure of the field and moved closer to its edge. As he eased along, he gave the surrounding brush a pass or two with his massive antlers. He felt the velvet, which now covered the antlers, begin to give a little, though the velvet would remain intact for a while longer.

At this point in the summer, he was as far away from his autumn self as he would get. For a brief period of time over the next few weeks, Essene would almost be totally free from the annual, paranoid eruptions of the mating season. This period was becoming increasingly rare because, as each year passed by, the pressures of the position that he held in the deer hierarchy would increase dramatically as he struggled to survive and propagate. Already, way down in the basement of his emotional being, Essene could feel the tide beginning to gather in preparation for the dark turning. But for today, in this year, he was able to accept the pleasure of the summer light.

He eased his face up to the last thin screen of hemlock needles which guarded the field's edge. He had smelt the shin-fa, and now that he was ready to step into the open, now Essene saw him. The shin-fa was at the further end of the field, digging the dirt as was their way, preparing the food for Essene and his kind that would be ready for them just in time to beef up in earnest for the mating season.

Essene had a healthy fear of the shin-fa. Of all the creatures which hunted and tried to kill him, the shin-fa were the most devious and dangerous. To look at them, one would not necessarily think that this would be the case, for they were tall and their mostly hairless, shiny faces shown like beacons when they walked through the leafless, autumn woods. But the shin-fa were persistent, and they could deal out death from a great distance. How they were able to achieve death without using neither fang nor claw, Essene never bothered to try to figure out. That they were able to do it was all he needed to know.

With their strange, dark, moveable horns, the shin-fa brought thunder to autumn even during bright, sunny days. As a matter of fact, no matter what the weather brought, be it rain, snow or fog, whenever Essene heard the sound of the shin-fa thunder he was smart enough to realize that the hunt was on.

Twice in his life he had felt the air around him compress, or seen branches snap as the shin-fa thunder sought him out. He had thought that he had been clever and careful but the shin-fa had nearly killed him. Essene had smelt the blood of others who had not been so lucky or had otherwise been careless. He saw the gut piles just before the crows and ravens had descended to clean them up, and, whether by luck or by design, he had learned from the misfortune of others— had learned to accurately read the myriad signs that the forest provided to him. Thus, most of the time, Essene was able to give the shin-fa a wide berth when they were on the hunt.

The squirrels' distant scold, the jays' raucous scream of hopeful betrayal, the thunderous eruption of an adult male grouse from the apparent safety of a thick fir stand in the middle of nowhere, these were the sounds which piqued his interest as he tried to rest in his lair during the rut. When these types of commotions came to him during his half-dreams, his big eyes would slide open, and he would begin to smell. Without moving at first, his experienced nose would start to take in the tentacles of truth contained in the scents which came to him along the forest floor. Sound and sight mattered, but it was his ability to decipher the troubling aspects of a faint, distant scent which served him well and set him apart from most other deer.

All of his kind were blessed with a keen sense of smell, but Essene had more to work with then most of his brethren. His antlers were huge, his body weight was huge (more than 300 lbs., live weight), and his nasal passages were larger than normal, relative to body size. Most importantly of all however, his brain, proportionally speaking, was ever so slightly larger than his counterparts. When those exaggerated nasal passages captured the distant presence of danger, his mature mind instantly went to work fabricating different scenarios that he might act upon should that distant danger proceed to disintegrate into an imminent one.

But that danger was not present now. Essene could see, hear and smell the shin-fa working at the other end of the long field. A slight southerly breeze carried the man's scent strongly up to Essene's nose. He knew this man, had smelt him before when the sun was coldly positioned behind a leafless mountain which blocked the northerly winds of fall. Essene had always been courageous, but he had felt dread that day. Essene respected this particular shin-fa for the concern that this man had been able to thrust into Essene's heart that frigid, November afternoon.

But the sun was warm now, and the shin-fa was not on the hunt. Still, Essene had never liked being seen by any shin-fa, under any circumstances. Instinct told him that it was a mistake to go into that field, but the axis of his life was turning, and he was strangely helpless to resist the pull of the doe and fawn feeding there. He moved forward.

–CHAPTER 5–

Earl "Scanty" Scott was usually a kind and gentle man, except when he was playing cribbage. He pretended to play for fun, mostly, but every so often the friendly tavern he frequented would have a not-so-friendly tournament. He always smiled when he started playing, but it wasn't long before the shadows and the frowns ruled completely.

Using a time-tested technique along with an extraordinary dose of perpetual good luck, Earl would usually waste little time in mugging his way to the top. The prizes he won never amounted to too much, but he always found each victory immensely satisfying. Reaffirming one's integral store of latent good luck could never be done frequently enough as far as Earl was concerned. Gambling wasn't a huge factor in his life but being able to gauge, to a reasonable degree, the role that patience played in making luck was a key to how Earl grew to measure things.

And, while cribbage was largely played for fun, poker, on the other hand, was another matter altogether. Once a month he landed at a table with six or seven old "friends." A congenial affair at first, it didn't take long before the game settled into a pot or no-limit affair.

They had been playing for over twenty years. There was very little about each other that they could not accurately read almost instantly. Patience had to be practiced astutely, traps laid with malignant care, and good, well-concealed hands had to be maximized to the highest degree possible.

The most recent game had been particularly brutal on Earl's psyche. In the evening's most decisive game he had drawn to a full boat with aces over jacks. None of the other players had seemed to be very proud of their hands, so Earl had emerged from his psychological cave to wager a large bet. Carey Fontaine saw the bet and promptly raised it the same amount. All of Earl's inner alarms were screaming, but he couldn't help himself. He re-raised one more time. Carey called and the cards were then laid on the table. Carey had four fives.

"Tough break there, Scanty," breathed Carey,

using Earl's old nickname with an obviously uncharitable relish.

Suddenly all of Earl's good works and a lifetime of mostly upright living was reduced to an unreasonably depraved level, in his own mind at least. The four fives seemed to magnify his nickname in a truly astonishing fashion. It was a real master stroke on Carey's part. Earl tried to shrug his shoulders in a nonchalant manner. It was important that the others did not see that Carey's use of the old nickname had unsettled him somehow. He was mostly successful in that regard, but his luck never did recover that evening.

The truth of the matter was that Earl didn't care for his nickname, but, as is usually the case, his friends paid no attention to his squeamishness in this regard. The devil was in the details.

He had been faithfully married for ages, but for one very brief period as a young man, he, angular, rugged and handsome, had unfairly, it seemed to him, acquired the reputation of being something of a rake. He had, truth be told, run wildly amuck through the countryside, finding himself beside as many willing females as he could. Most of them had been as young as he, though not all. More often than not, no matter what their age, most of them would in fact end up scantily clad indeed. Thus the nickname and its unwanted legacy was born. He tried thereafter to warn all the youngsters about this sort of behavior, to no avail.

Anyway, the day after the disastrous poker game, in an attempt at atonement, he went up to his vegetable garden to do battle with the hefty pigweeds which were taking control there. At first he somewhat angrily slashed at them with the hoe, doing only a cursory job at best. When he reached the first row of potatoes however, he switched gears.

Earl was a good gardener and he loved fresh potatoes. Good gardening required a great deal of effort, so it wasn't long before he flipped the hoe aside and got down on his hands and knees to extract the large weeds by hand. As the rows were very long, this practice of hand-weeding was very beneficial to someone attempting to restore a measure of patience and good grace back into their life. Given the size and number of pigweed, Earl had to grudgingly admit to himself that after all, maybe it was a good thing that he had lost at poker the night before. He thought of how much money he had lost. Sweat began to run to the tip of his sharp, hawk-like nose.

He hadn't won at cribbage lately either, and he was beginning to be seriously concerned that his current store of good luck might be all used up. Then, halfway up the second row of potatoes, he glanced up.

There, right in the middle of the field, right in the middle of the day, was a big doe eating clover with a fawn caprioling without a care in the world. Instinctively, Earl lowered himself behind the weeds and potatoes to keep from being seen.

Earl was good at quite a few things. He was a good gardener, a good poker and cribbage player, as well as a reasonably good husband and father. But the thing which he really devoted himself to, as much as he could anyway, for he was a working man and therefore didn't have a whole lot of free time, the thing he really devoted himself to more than anything else was deer hunting.

Seeing the doe and fawn out in the open like that was a good sign. *Maybe*, he thought, *maybe my luck is going to change.*

What he saw next would leave him no doubt that his run of bad luck was over. Without any concern whatsoever, just like that little fawn, the most magnificent buck Earl had ever seen in his life, with his massive, velvet covered horns reaching high above his regal head, stepped out into the open vastness of the field to watch the fawn frolic.

–CHAPTER 6–

Phyla viewed Essene's emergence into the field with a certain amount of alarm. This was definitely outside the realm of normalcy. For a buck such as Essene to expose himself to open observation to a shin-fa was an event that she had never witnessed before. Her tail twitched involuntarily, giving away her considerable apprehension.

She herself was not concerned by the repeated presence of female or young shin-fa, as long as they stayed at the far end of the field fooling with the garden. But she didn't enjoy the attention that she and her fawn were obviously receiving from time to time as the apparently innocuous male shin-fa labored down below them. His very presence radiated a certain, dormant aggression which was never to be totally ignored, even though he wasn't on the hunt.

However, the heat from the summer sun

kept down the number of flies and other pests which were perpetually plaguing her and her solitary fawn. The feed in the field at this time of year was rich and full, though somewhat bland. The garden that the shin-fa was laboring in wouldn't be ready to attract her attention for at least another month yet. But there was another reason not to dismiss a beneficial aspect the relatively close proximity of the dreaded shin-fa provided her.

Early that morning, when the rising sun had shifted the wind a bit, Phyla had detected the possibility that a pack of coydogs might be lurking nearby. It was nothing concrete like an actual sighting, but an alert, intelligent doe like Phyla always did everything in her power to avoid even the possibility of a contact with those vile and remorseless creatures. She had abandoned the vicinity of the remote meadow that she had been hanging around, kept the wind in her favor, and made a direct run to this field where, experience had taught her, some shin-fa might provide their odious and violent shield against the dreaded coydogs.

When she finally arrived at the field and realized that it was a non-hunting, male shin-fa who was going to provide her and her fawn with protection, she wasn't entirely happy at first, but after a while, she allowed herself to relax and enjoy the moment. Essene's arrival ruined all that.

Her first reaction when she saw him enter the field was to freeze, while surveying the dense woods behind him for any flickering, hunting movement. She flared her nostrils, gathering scent while the hair in her erect ears filtered the stillness for some sound which would indicate a restless, hungry energy in the green shadows behind Essene.

Almost in the same instance, her eyes scanned and strove to interpret Essene's body language for signs of tenseness or even, in the case of an imminent coydog attack—even fear.

Phyla's breeding and genetics were every bit as impressive as the massive buck now facing her. It took her about two seconds to assess the situation. Whereas before she had twitched her tail in apprehension at Essene's arrival, now she flicked it about momentarily in an involuntary gesture of annoyance.

It wasn't the breeding season. There was no reason to concern herself with Essene one way or the other. But she could not quite pull off her desire to display a total indifference to the father of her fawn. He had committed an unspeakable breach of etiquette by entering this open space with her and her fawn present. She could feel the hot excitement in the male shin-fa's gaze when he ceased his work to drool at the spectacle of Essene.

Essene, being a male, was totally uncon-cerned with Phyla's unseemly apprehension. As for the distant shin-fa, well, the garden appeared to be rounding into top shape for a fantastic future feed.

–CHAPTER 7–

Lois was, she felt, nearly bored to death. The worst part was she felt with a searing, unrelenting sort of despair—the worst part was that the whole thing was her own fault! She could have put off the laundry for another day but no . . . no, no, no, no!

Instead, she had rudely informed her then-sane husband that the garden was approaching a cataclysmic state of irreversible weed infestation, and that he had to take care of it immediately, while she caught up on what she felt was an equally cataclysmic laundry condition. Now she had to pay the price for her inexplicable rashness.

When he had returned from the garden later that afternoon he was largely incoherent. Attacking yet another mountain of underwear and stockings, Lois initially had missed the telltale signs of mental instability when her husband had staggered to the kitchen table and began babbling about some sort of miraculous vision which had been visited upon him as he labored in the lowly earth of the garden.

Some of what he initially talked about Lois understood.

However, when Earl began to describe, with unrestrained rapture, not only the height of the G-2s, but their girth as well, Lois felt the fine hairs on the back of her neck rise with apprehension. She had been scrutinizing a pair of Earl's old underwear, trying to decide whether or not to fold them or relegate them to the dusting pile. She carefully backed away from the dryer. Once she had gotten to what she felt to be a safe distance away from her husband, she then turned to lean up against the counter to face him.

He was sitting at the kitchen table, absently cuffing away at the sandwich she had left there for him. His eyes were looking toward her, but they were glazed over and decidedly, disconcertingly, unfocused.

"Pretty big deer huh?" she said more then asked, as she folded her arms with the slightest hint of boredom.

The question, posed as it was, contained just enough implied sarcasm to press a few hidden buttons which she had developed for calculated use in a twenty-two year old marriage. It worked!

With almost an audible click, Earl's mind reacted to his wife's latent anger. His dark blue eyes, which had been locked on some obscure middle ground, turned ever so briefly black with rage as he quickly glanced at her and then looked away. As usual, she was right and he was wrong. Would it never end?

"Yeah," he said, recovering his composure, "I hope the hell he never takes a liking to string beans. He'd eat the whole damn bunch in one sittin'."

"You need a haircut bad," replied Lois good-naturedly. "I'll save the clippings, mix 'em with some soap, and you can spread it around the edge of the garden this weekend."

"Might work, though I got a feeling that guy does pretty much what he wants, when he wants," said Earl.

Lois saw an opening and quickly went into the adjoining room to retrieve her clippers and plastic cape. Earl always acted poorly when his hair got long, so she about strangled him when she wrapped the plastic cape around his neck just as he was saying, "I never had any idea an animal of that size lived around here."

–CHAPTER 8–

He had sort of forgotten about it until now. Not that any deer hunter ever really forgets anything about deer hunting. After a hard, cold day out in the field, every deer hunter's wife can attest to the curse once a robust amount of beer or, God forbid, whiskey has been consumed during the post-supper poker game.

Every nuance, every subtlety of the day's events slip out from every hunter, slowly at first, then with more and more conviction as each hunter's individual story acts to reinforce all the other stories, until the murky puzzle of the day's hunt becomes irrevocably intertwined into a great mosaic which clearly depicts the deepest meaning of life itself. Naturally, by morning's first light all is forgotten.

But Earl was not under the influence of any foreign substances when he received this particular piece of the hunting puzzle. He had been very young, and his grandfather was still alive. Once he was old enough, he had been allowed to go out hunting with his uncles and with his father, without a gun of course, and had managed to comport himself very well.

His grandfather had noticed this and had decided to impart to him a small pearl of wisdom. It had been shady and cool in the woodshed where they—his grandfather and he—had been repairing the handle of an axe. Earl didn't know much about living at that age, but he did know one thing, when grandfather talked, you had better get busy listening.

Now, many years later, Earl was almost scared when he recalled with startling clarity that particular episode. The stark morning light had cut across the cold blueness of his grandfather's right eye as it fixed upon his grandson and held him as he spoke.

"Up beyond the lower field," he stated flatly, "not far beyond the second stone wall, is an ancient, ancient game trail. My father told me about it. It's all grown up, it all looks the same, but when the big deer travel, that's where they come through. "

Thereafter, Earl had hunted that general area quite a bit, but usually he ended up deeper into the woods, "further up," as he would put it. There, not too far from a large apple orchard and the fields of two dairy farms, a series of ridges converged into a large hollow. Deer, at times, seemed to be funneled there, and he had had some success sitting there over the years. But he had never seen any large bucks, only their tracks where they had passed through the night before.

Earl often wondered why this was so. Why, all things being equal, why hadn't a monster buck presented itself at least once during all those hours he had sat there in early morning or late in the afternoon? Was it just bad luck, or was something else at work there?

Through the years, Earl had noticed that some very impressive bucks had shown up in his area late in the season. He knew this because of the snow which usually had arrived at that time of the year. It was generally quite cold then, so sitting as a hunting technique had been abandoned in favor of still hunting. Even the slight careful movements involved in still hunting were enough to keep a hunter warm compared to trying to sit for long periods of time on a frigid November day.

Earl would still hunt through his early season sitting area, but he would no longer sit there in the late afternoon because he wanted to be closer to the warmth of home at the end of the day. He knew how to accurately read a track in the snow. After a few years, it was apparent to him that spending time in his early season sitting area would have been a waste of time later in the season. Deer would pass through there in the evening hours but never during the day. Their patterns had changed.

But the snow told a different story about the general area his grandfather had been referring to all those years ago. Big tracks would show up there late in the season once in a while. Besides, it was close enough to home to encourage some serious sitting time. After sitting in the cold for a long period of time it was always nice to be as close to the warmth of the hearth as possible. After seeing the big buck in the field that summer, Earl decided that he would have to invest some serious money into some good, cold-weather clothing and dedicate some precious late-season hunting time to justify the purchase of that clothing.

But the problem remained as to where exactly the ancient game trail that he had been referring to was located. Earl's grandfather had been generously sparse when it came to specific details in this regard. It was enough, he felt, to point the kid in the right direction. Why get all hung up on details? The fact that he had no idea whatsoever where the exact location of the trail was, was immaterial. If his grandson was a true hunter, then he would figure it out.

Since Earl had seen the buck, he had spent a lot of time ruminating and rolling around a large amount of details about the territory, which was supposed to contain this—by now mythical—game trail. Then, sitting at the breakfast table one morning, something clicked.

Not too far from where he lived, the main river of the region drained a vast area of the surrounding foothills. This had been going on since the last ice-age, some ten thousand years ago. Every fall there were two places along that river which held a certain type of mushroom which Earl collected to help pay the taxes. This required a lot of walking through regions which had no tote roads due to wet areas or steep banks. The best way to navigate this terrain was to follow the old deer trails. They cut right into the banks and were easy to walk along if a man exercised due diligence and care.

Of course, being along a main river, which acted as a territorial boundary, meant that these trails were much more heavily traveled than was the norm. Earl could think of no such obvious trails where his grandfather had been talking about, but that didn't necessarily mean that his grandfather had been in error.

Earl knew that sitting along main trails was alright if you wanted to shoot a doe or skipper. However, when snow was on the ground he could see that older, more experienced bucks eschewed the use of main trails, except at night. When the height of the rut was on, sometimes big bucks would make mistakes and get shot, but on the whole, the trails that the big bucks used were their own trails. These trails, generally speaking, always drove through thick cover, were apparently totally random, and were always around the periphery of where a local herd of deer might be residing.

Earl would, as he grew older, occasionally take a sort of perverse pleasure at realizing that the longer he hunted, the more that he thought he knew about deer and their ways, that there would always come a moment in the season when he would realize that he knew nothing whatsoever about these beautiful, magnificent creatures. But that fact never once stopped him from imagining that he could, if he applied himself thoroughly, get a leg up on these critters. This was such a moment. Had he not seen the buck? Had the animal not displayed himself in the full light of the day? Something was afoot. Earl had no illusions of ever even remotely comprehending why such an experienced animal had chosen to reveal his presence the way he did. But that didn't mean that Earl would not do everything in his admittedly limited power to take advantage of the situation. The deer was here for some reason. Earl didn't care what the reason was as long as it put him in the right place at the right time.

Earl rattled his coffee cup back onto his saucer and prepared to get up from the table. Lois, who had been chattering mindlessly at the kitchen sink doing dishes, caught something of an agitation in the air when the cup met the saucer. She turned her head slightly toward her husband.

"Bring those over here if you're done with 'em," she requested pleasantly enough to bring an edge of caution into Earl's demeanor.

He did as she asked and was rewarded by having her lean up against him slightly when he deposited the dishes into the sink. It worked. Now he could not lie to her, not completely anyway.

"What are you up to this morning?" she asked a bit warmly, turning her calm green eyes up to meet his truculent blue ones.

"Oh I guess I'll go up to see if we've got any beans left," he replied easily enough, seeing as it was "sort of" true. He was essentially helpless now.

He noticed a small, dark cloud swiftly pass over those pretty green eyes, but at the same instant he realized that he was in the clear. Still, he knew something more was coming, so he stayed in place looking at her.

"You've still got some of your hair left in the drawer there," she said in a neutral sort of voice. "Take some up and spread it around the edges. That'll take care of that deer."

He ignored her apparent use of the singular and pressed on to gain more time. "I'll probably weed a little and then go up to see what I want to cut for firewood next winter," he added as offhandedly as he could, though he could see that she wasn't believing any of it.

She had greeted this last remark with a sudden, icy silence, so he gave her arm a gentle squeeze, her cheek a small peck, and then he turned with a certain, lingering feeling of bewilderment and left the room. On the way out the door he had to admit to himself that while he didn't know much about deer, he knew even less about his wife.

–CHAPTER 9–

Earl decided to walk up to the field where the garden was located. This was a journey of over half a mile, but he didn't mind because the day was sunny, breezy, and just plain pleasant. On the way up he decided that he would tend to the garden later in the afternoon. First he had to settle something in his mind before hunting season got any closer.

Just before he got to the field containing his garden, the road along which he was walking became heavily shaded by the white maple, gray birch and white pine which had finally managed to crowd out the last vestiges of the worn-out pastures that his grandfather had attempted to utilize when maintaining whatever cattle that he had been keeping at the time.

Over the years, Earl had used these woods to his advantage when he was hunting. The road came into the field at an angle, with a small portion of the field below him to his left, and the majority extending up above him to his right. Moving carefully, Earl could approach the field undetected and get a look, first at the small portion and then, after a few more tentative steps, at the broad expanse of most of the right-hand part of the field. However, a slight knoll three hundred yards up near the woods did prevent him from viewing the whole field cleanly. Four times he had shot deer doing this.

Earl didn't like spooking deer ahead of hunting season, so most of the time when he was walking along this road he would just barge right out into the field to go about his business, whether it be gardening, fishing, gathering wild strawberries or wild mushrooms. If deer were nearby fooling with the garden, then Earl didn't mind it one bit if they bounded off into the woods with alarm and consternation.

After all they had no business being there, and, with a lot of luck, the sudden fright might keep them out of the garden to some extent. Earl never counted on that eventuality very much however. Usually soap, mothballs, or a packet of human hair, like the one he now carried in his pocket, would be spread around the perimeter of the garden to keep various critters out of it long enough to keep the vegetables alive until they were ready to be harvested.

Today however, Earl found himself slowing down as he approached a line of young fir trees which guarded the road's entry into the field. After all he was just pretending to be gardening and he was wondering if maybe . . . .

A quick glance to his left told him that that part of the field was clear. The breeze was in his favor, so as he edged his head around the last furry fir tree and peered up the right-hand side. He half expected to witness the presence of the majestic animal he had seen three weeks before. He was almost disappointed when he realized that this was not the case.

The thought, *I'll never see him again,* flashed through his mind as he abandoned his stealth mode and hustled up past the garden, dropping his packet of hair between the final row of corn and the first row of beans as he did so.

Yes, the garden needed some work after he got around to spreading the hair properly, but for the next few hours he had other fish to fry. Earl headed out for the woods bordering the upper part of the field. Not too far beyond those woods lay the stonewalls which his grandfather had been referring to when he was a child.

Four hundred yards from the garden he cut up to his left when the woods drew near. There was an old tote road here which would lead him close to the first of the two stonewalls in question. The second stonewall was only a hundred yards beyond this one, but it was invisible due to a thick stand of mostly young fir and hemlock.

The first stonewall was still in good shape. It consisted of a stout base of large boulders topped off by a generous layer of smaller stones, as the former field or pasture had been smoothed out for use.

The second wall was, as was often the case in remote areas of old farms, in a state of disrepair which bordered on it nearly disappearing into the forest floor. One could almost see the elderly farmer losing his courage in the face of some monstrous inevitability that only he could appreciate. Or maybe, after a lifetime of building and repairing these walls, maybe he simply didn't feel the need to be overly fancy this far back.

Earl often wondered why there had been a need for two stonewalls way back here in the woods anyway. Something about funneling cattle from one area to another he always figured, but with the forest now so fully grown, it was difficult to visualize the function of the stonewalls with any degree of certainty.

It was all a little gloomy if you dwelled on it too much, and Earl wasn't about to make that mistake now. He found an easy crossing point in the dilapidated second wall, and then he headed for a huge rock on the other side. Other than the rock, he had no idea what he was looking for. In logical terms, Earl would have thought that wildlife would have sought out the same corridor that the farmer had closed off with his two stonewalls. But as he approached the giant rock, it occurred to Earl that good husbandry probably had nothing in common with the impulses of wildlife which had recently been liberated from an age of ice.

Looking at it objectively, Earl had to admit that the land beyond the second stonewall was difficult. Suddenly the giant rock no longer mattered to him except, perhaps, as a point of reference in the coming fall. The land he was standing on was what he felt to be important. The word that came to his mind was, s*table— this ground is stable.*

The spot where the giant rock sat marked the end of this "stable" area. Earl knew that beyond this point the ground sloped gradually but persistently downhill for a long way, maybe a mile or more. He turned to face northwest with his left shoulder parallel with the stonewalls. Though he had passed through this place many times over the years, it was as if only now was he really seeing it for the first time.

Beyond the screen of the forest ahead of him, this "stable" area he was standing on ran for a long way toward the boundary of the farm. That boundary consisted of a small, swift-flowing brook which was well hidden in a deep gorge. Beyond that gorge was an extensive foothill which was situated right smack in the center of this section of woods. There were roads all around this block of woods, but most of them were barely big enough to hold the asphalt which covered them. They were back roads that any deer worth its salt could leap over with no effort.

Suddenly Earl gave a shallow gasp as he realized what he was seeing. On either side of this particular foothill, on the other side of these particular back roads, were very large tracts of uninhabited forest. There might be a few fields or logging roads poking into them, but by and large, these tracts of land, because of their mountainous, inhospitable nature, stretched for miles in uninterrupted splendor.

In the fall, just before deer season, Earl had spent many years roaming through the woods collecting wild mushrooms. At the first of the season when he would come onto his secret spots, the ground would always look the same, and for a little while he would have a difficult time finding his quarry. But Earl was an experienced mushroom hunter, and it wouldn't be long before he found his "mushroom eyes."

Soon he could look quite a ways off and easily spot the variations in the littered forest floor which would indicate the locations of mushrooms even before they came out of the ground. One simply had to concentrate and focus on the task at hand.

It was the same now. Standing there facing the invisible foothill, Earl perceived that he was standing on the tip of a very large gear. That gear extended up through the foothill and intertwined, right and left, with the genetic gears extending out of those large tracts of land beyond the surrounding back roads. For whatever reason known only to nature, whenever these gigantic gears turned, the big bucks would come to keep the blood fresh and ready for generations of improvement. That's what that big buck had been checking up on.

Earl glanced at the big rock to his right. No need to worry about it today. He decided that anywhere in around here would be fine when the time came.

–CHAPTER 10–

The lure of the edge is strong. From time immemorial deer have relied on edges. The edge of any clearing, manmade or otherwise, is where most deer make their living. Here is where the tender, nutritious vegetation they need grows in relative abundance. It is also the place where all their predators will be apt to lurk.

A clearing in the forest is a double edged sword which serves both the hunter and the hunted equally well. The edges provide the contact points around which the current of the forest ebb and flow in a perpetual game of give and take. Whoever reads that current correctly will live on.

As a result of some tragedy suffered long before the birth of Sejanus by one of his highly intelligent and perhaps overly sensitive ancestors, open areas such as fields were regarded with the full measure of terror that they deserved.

Perhaps with more than they deserved because, as time went by, the tribe that Sejanus descended from retreated further and further up into the remotest parts of the white-tail kingdom. Only the mechanics of genetics and the absolute need for food could pull them reluctantly out of their mountain hideaway.

When the nearby convenience of the available gene pool would begin to clog up, then a certain number of their tribe would feel the inexplicable need to slip away during the breeding season and go down into the far away valleys and fields. There, after several generations, some of their number would follow that same inexplicable need right back up to the remote crags to nudge or violently shove a stagnating gene pool back into balance.

It is all a somewhat delicate interplay of conflicting forces. Though the danger of living around an apparent edge is less in the remote crags, so is there, however, less of an opportunity to broaden one's biological base. Deer in the highlands might tend to become too interbred, become too paranoid, and therefore too vulnerable to having their genetic line terminated. Fortunately for the deer of these types of areas, the mast crop can provide a level playing field in an otherwise uneven mating game.

It is perhaps no accident of nature that during the mating season, when deer are most susceptible to being killed by their enemies, that a significant mast crop can tip the balance decidedly in favor of the deer. The nuts of beech and oak trees allow deer to feed randomly anywhere they want in the forest, thus eliminating a lot of the dangers that are posed by incessantly hanging round the edges of fields and roads. Indeed, the presence of an abundant mast crop will set off a delicate trigger within even the most remote white-tail tribe. Besides the obvious factor of having a large, readily available source of winter fat dumped into their laps, there were other less obvious benefits to having a large mast crop.

When the deer from the lowlands show up to chow down on the beloved beechnuts and acorns, it isn't all sweetness and light. There are plenty of pinned-back ears and angry stomping of feet as the resident deer express their latent disapproval of the invasion of their territory by the opportunistic flatland cousins. However, if the mast crop is truly abundant then there won't be too much ear wringing or squabbling.

Though the highland deer are more used to living on the edge and are therefore more prone to being overprotective of their limited resources, instinct nevertheless provides them with a certain amount of decorum and good manners. After all, the mast isn't good every year and even if it is good, it won't last all year. At some point, the highland deer always have to venture beyond their territory to get food. Simply put, one of the major benefits to having a good mast crop is the fostering of social contacts with other groups of deer. In the years of plenty, the deer party-hearty and get to know each other a little bit. Even the most paranoid and anti-social highland deer would be better tolerated down below if they kept their cool up above during the times of plenty.

There is one other thing regarding the triggering mechanism of a large mast crop. Whenever the beechnuts and acorns blanket the highlands, the doe of those regions go from having one fawn a year to having two or even three fawn. It could simply be the presence of plenty which encourages this, but more than likely the increased birthrate is a combination of things. When the mast is plentiful and the lowland herd moves in to feed on it, the highland doe react by increasing their own numbers to protect their territorial imperative.

So mast crops are wonderful when they occur, and, generally speaking, the bigger the trees in the forest, the more nuts that will fall from them. But this is the trouble with remote, rugged areas: the more hassle it is for landowners and loggers to get to the wood, the harder it is cut when harvesting time comes around.

In the highlands, because of all the ice storms and the poor soil, the wood, though large, is frequently of poor quality. And, even if the wood is of good value, it might be miles from any place to land it where a truck can get to it.

And they aren't easy miles either. Bony, steep, saturated with hidden spring holes erupting out of rotten ledge, the ground-holding highland wood is just the kind of place a logger only wants to visit once per lifetime. The selective cutting process here is quite elemental: anything worth taking, take it.

This, of course, is bad news for the mast crop. Deer can sometimes see their whole territories destroyed as far as acorns and beechnuts are concerned. If the ground is steep enough and the soil poor enough, it might be a hundred years before any significant mast returns. These severe clear cuts, after twenty or thirty years, can offer some sustenance and shelter, but, on the whole, these areas are places where deer travel through to get to a place that can still offer a mast crop or a distant, green field. A thirty-year-old clear cut was where Sejanus was brought up.

A blasted, savaged, ruinous landscape had, over those thirty years, managed to heal itself enough to encourage the mother of Sejanus to hold court there despite all the negatives inherent in such a situation. The old clear cut was sufficiently barren, sufficiently nondescript enough to encourage an intelligent and resourceful mother to raise her most important offspring amongst its unremarkable embrace. But it did have one distinct disadvantage however: it required travel.

–CHAPTER 11–

Sejanus frequently dreamed of his mother. Seldom were these dreams entirely pleasant. A dominant, paranoid doe, the mother of Sejanus lived in the most remote part of one of the largest, unbroken stretches of forest in western Maine. This made her life an incredibly difficult proposition. Finding enough food for her and her offspring was never a sure thing. Even obtaining water in the mountainous crags which made up her home base was sometimes a chore which required her to stray further from her comfort zone then she really wanted to. But she had learned from her own mother the virtues of remoteness and solitude, and she pursued those virtues with an enthusiasm and an intelligence which reflected well on the character of her forebears.

In fact, becoming a forebear showed a remarkable persistence in and of itself. Indeed, of all the problems confronting Sejanus' mother, the most serious ones presented themselves when the breeding season rolled around. Her genetic makeup was highly desirable, but she lived on the very outer edge of white-tail society. Desirable bucks usually would not be able to come to her. She had to go to them.

In her territory there were several faint, obscure fingers of adjacent white-tail claims which, every year, she would have to gingerly probe into when looking for a buck. If she moved too quickly or carelessly, she would occasionally come in conflict with the ruling matriarch of that particular adjacent area. Then she would have to decide whether to fight for what was available there or flee. Usually she fled to avoid possible injury at the hooves of an enraged matriarch.

All this probing and avoidance made her a late breeder. This disposition to breed late was not entirely a learned behavior. She lived where she did because several generations of her ancestors had felt the same way about things. Breeding late was one of her most important genetic tools for surviving and propagating.

Usually by the time the urge to breed was strongly upon her, at least some of the surrounding matriarchs had already been quickened by a roving buck. If such was the case, then she would no longer be viewed as much of a threat. In fact, being pregnant would encourage these matriarchs to avoid conflict with her. This gave her some sort of opportunity to find whatever bucks were left around.

This unfortunate circumstance presented another problem, perhaps the most overriding problem of all. Most bucks of any consequence whatsoever went to and fought over the biggest genetic pool they could horn in on. Doe on the outermost fringes of the white-tail world had to make do with whatever stumbled their way. Usually this was a very serious matter.

For her whole life, the mother of Sejanus had to mate with inferior or immature bucks of questionable lineage. Some of them were scarcely more than spike-horns. Over the course of time, this tended to make her even more short-tempered and paranoid than she already was naturally. She was running out of opportunities and, instinctively, she knew it. She was approaching the end of her prime.

Then, after a series of extremely hard, cold winters, the great gears of the white-tail world sprang into action in an attempt to balance the losses incurred as a result of those winters. The following autumn would be important.

She was extremely anxious that fall. The unmistakable tension of extinction was in the air. It had always been hard before, what now?

As it turned out, she and the white-tail world didn't have to worry. As concerned as she had been, she still didn't come into heat any earlier then she normally did, which made her chances of happening on a buck somewhat slim, so it would seem.

However, just as she was beginning to make her first delicate foray into a neighboring territory, a great crash amongst the young fir and hemlock in front of her brought her to an abrupt standstill.

Ordinarily such a commotion would have sent a paranoid creature such as herself into a headlong flight, but for some reason she held her ground against the impending approach of what surely had to be an unmitigated disaster. The crashing did subside just a tad as whatever was before her continued to unapologetically barge through the wild and ineffective brush. Her eyes were plenty wide open when the most magnificent specimen of white-tail manhood she had ever seen came at her with his head down and shaking his unbelievable massive antlers by way of introduction and demanding a quick and immediate surrender to his will. Well then, who was she to argue? This was the father of Sejanus—a master buck of the first order.

–CHAPTER 12–

There are some who might say that the mating of the father and mother of Sejanus was the result of nothing but sheer luck and blind instinct. A big, dominant buck had been aimlessly, desperately, wandering around and had simply happened upon a receptive doe where he had least expected to. The only reason that he had been in that area at all was because the previous two winters had been very severe and had seriously reduced the deer herd, the skeptics would maintain. Ordinarily, these doubters would forcefully assert that ordinarily the mother of Sejanus would have been left out in the cold, genetically speaking, and that she had simply been the recipient of a generous dose of good fortune when the father of Sejanus had shown up.

But what exactly did the high death toll of the previous winters trigger within the bosom of

Sejanus' father? Some would maintain that the father knew exactly where he was going when he headed out for the home territory of Sejanus' mother. That's why he didn't beat around the bush when he got himself near her. Some would say that this buck's great-grandfather or great-aunt or great-something-or-other had either come from this place or had been aware of the relatively important position that this area held in this particular corner of the white-tail universe.

Some would say that there are many things which influence the movements of certain white-tail groups. A large river may act as a barrier or a guidepost, depending on any number of extenuating circumstances. The beginning or ending of any particular agricultural zone is apt to squeeze groups of deer in one direction or another, depending on rainfall, food, or the high death toll of severe winters.

The father of Sejanus was responding to a deep pool of genetic knowledge in response to a specific situation. Deer are not created equal. Between the numskulls on the bottom and the master bucks on the top is a huge differential which is not readily apparent. The gene pools of the various deer groups work their way back and forth in a greasy, uneven manner which, though fluid, is nevertheless an unbreakable mechanism which allows for the kind of adaptation which ensures the survival of the species.

However, though both the top and bottom layers of the white-tail society are, as a practical matter, both important, they are not equal. As a rule the numskulls and their close associates are the ones who get shot or eaten by coydogs. If they don't get eaten or shot, then the descendants of these lower echelons might, over time, rise up through the ranks to the highest levels of white-tail society. Everything is a circle.

It must be said that the number of master bucks is very minute. Only a tiny percentage of male deer occupy this realm. There are good bucks, big bucks, and then there are master bucks. Master bucks are, without doubt, crucial members of the herd. They apply the pressure which forces the genetic grease into the places which allow the herd, as a whole, to adapt and survive. Age will depose a master buck but rarely will a bullet do so.

Indeed, most master bucks live out their natural lives in the woods. Some, in the more remote areas, might live out their existence without being detected by even the most astute hunters. Paranoid, unusually intelligent, and diligent, some of these deer seldom leave scrapes and only occasionally will rub a six- or eight-inch tree in an obscure area away from trails or anything else which would apparently indicate something important.

This was how the father of Sejanus operated. He was a line buck who traveled light and knew what he wanted when he wanted it. He chose the mother of Sejanus because of some genetic signal that she was projecting at the time. She was exactly what he wanted.

Yes, when Sejanus dreamt of his mother, the dreams were usually unpleasant, because she was domineering and demanding. She had been that way with all her offspring, but with Sejanus she had taken it to a new level. Though she probably would, like all mothers, protest that all her offspring were equally important to her, the fact of the matter was that Sejanus was her favorite, plain and simple.

He had come to her during an important moment in her own life when her twin attributes of high fertility and extreme physical prowess were at their peak. It may well be that she recognized in him her best chance of passing on her own genetic blueprint, of leaving her stamp on the white-tail race. Even as a young fawn, Sejanus displayed a physical and psychological presence which aroused in her a fiercely protective and anxious manner which would never subside until the day Sejanus had to take out on his own.

This extreme parental behavior on the part of his mother might have ruined lesser youngsters, but not Sejanus. He was made from very stern stuff. When she came down on him hard, he was intelligent enough to realize that there must be a good reason for it. He never resented her being harsh with him when the occasion called for harshness. Any such resentment would have indicated a commonness which he did not possess. His father had given him the ability to absorb and to learn things quickly and dispassionately. His mother recognized this capacity in him and she piled it on. The days and nights were too short but she gave it everything she had, and she had a lot.

At first, during his early months, his mother kept him close to his place of birth. Every nook and cranny of their remote home was explored, when she deemed it safe enough for him to be out and about. The ways and means of going from one place to another in those remote crags was inexhaustibly gone over again and again as she taught him how to use various aspects of the land to its greatest advantage. To use the seemingly obvious routes to confound, confuse, and ultimately lose those who would do him harm was something she did with pinned ears on a daily basis.

Finally, after he had grown a little and was sufficiently bonded to her, finally she took him down off the crags to show him where food and water were more readily available. It also meant that there would be other fawns to play with and learn from. This was important because, after all, there was a pecking order to establish.

At this time of the year the respective matriarchs in these adjacent areas would tolerate Sejanus and his mother. There was safety in numbers in these remote regions as long as a certain decorum was observed. Sejanus' mother was obliged to display a reluctant, subservient manner toward the resident matriarch whenever she and Sejanus ventured into the immediate presence of a boss doe. This didn't happen very often because, again, the main reason for the journey was to show Sejanus the lay of the land and to expose him to his future competition. His mother had no objection to achieving this goal in as safe a manner as was possible. And the plan, as far as safety was concerned, was to have many deer eyes in a given vicinity without anyone needing to feel threatened. Having his mother get in a wrestling match with the resident matriarch was never part of the plan. If she had to withdraw to the extreme periphery of a resident matriarch's territory while Sejanus strutted his stuff, then she would do so without any apparent ill will whatsoever. It didn't bother her in the least to be left out of someone else's sewing circle. She had made a career out of being anti-social, and she had no intention of changing her ways now.

No, the mother of Sejanus didn't give two hoots about other deer. If she never saw another one as long as she lived then that would be just fine with her. This, in spite of the fact that some of the deer they came in contact with were directly descended from her, this was now an absolute truth as far as she was concerned: Sejanus was the only deer that she even remotely cared about.

Sejanus himself picked up on this somewhat unusual attitude of his mother's, and it showed when he interacted with the other fawns. The pecking order was quickly established wherever they went. Even at this early stage, Sejanus was already bigger, stronger and faster than his counterparts. Though bullied by his mother,

Sejanus himself wasn't a bully; he was simply a dominant individual who happened to have a very demanding teacher.

They didn't bother to linger too long in any one area. The minute any of the other doe began to display any obvious signs of annoyance toward their unwelcome guests, Sejanus would feel himself being scooted off by his mother. There were many other places to see and many more lessons that she had to impart to her son. He would be a seasoned traveler indeed by summer's end.

–CHAPTER 13–

After two months or so of wandering from one deer domain to another, Sejanus and his mother finally arrived at a very strange place. Sheltered by the usual dark thicket of young fir and hemlock, Sejanus became aware of an intense anxiety which had overtaken his mother.

Her ears were up and they were slowly, so as not to attract attention, slowly rotating on a tight axis as she went through the process of attempting to detect the possibility of something which could represent a danger. Her eyes were also wide open and her nose elevated as she utilized every sense she had to determine whether or not it was safe to move forward.

Usually at a time like this Sejanus was forbidden to fidget, but he was a bit older now and thus could be forgiven a certain amount of foolishness, especially when no concrete evidence of danger was forthcoming. His mother had moved up over him as they had come to the edge of this particular thicket, but now, though she was displaying all the signs of an unusual amount of caution, now his curiosity was getting the better of him. Slowly, the way she had taught him, slowly he edged his head out around her right front leg.

Not too far from where they stood, an openness of light he had never experienced before warmly beckoned to him and urged him to move closer. It was the first field he had ever seen. A long time passed before the open light softened with the setting of the summer sun. Finally his mother edged forward with her nose low to the ground to pick up any scent which might have gone undetected previously. She had known for a long time that it was safe, but it was important to her that she teach Sejanus the proper way to enter a dangerous place like the field in front of them.

Deer like to enter fields near a corner so that if something unexpected happens they can slip back into the woods as quickly as possible. Of course the trouble with entering near a corner was that you never can reliably tell what lay around that corner. It's a bad deal all the way around but it's better than being at the top of a hill in the middle of a field.

Corners offer emerging deer less light and a certain amount of natural camouflage, which they find somewhat reassuring. By such a corner, one that his mother had used the only other time she had been here, Sejanus entered the unbelievable beauty of an open field for the first time.

The alcove where they entered was created by a block of white maple and poplar trees, which intruded about thirty yards toward the center of the field. These trees grew on either side of a partially submerged stonewall which had been built around a wet bog hole. In the center of this boggy area a lot of young fir and pine grew, making it difficult to see through to the other side. The stonewall, forming an edge, followed the block of woods out into the field before abruptly ending. The woods kept going another fifteen yards beyond the wall's end and then turned right in a straight line a little over forty-five yards before gradually winging back to join back into the main block of woods. Though less well defined, the woods also created a corner on that side of the wet area.

Though the view of that corner was poor due to the fir and pine, Sejanus' mother was nevertheless able to detect a glimpse of some movement in that direction. She was not alarmed.

Upon seeing the movement, she instantly recognized it as belonging to other deer.

Due to the long, overhanging branches of mature beech trees, the area where Sejanus and his mother came out into the field had very sparse grass. This didn't pass muster with his mother, so Sejanus was encouraged to go further out into the field where the timothy grass was starting to get quite tall and therefore provided good cover for the fawn. Sejanus, once given the green light, didn't need a lot of encouragement to take full advantage of the wide open spaces. Pretty soon he was blasting about the landscape, heading nowhere and everywhere at the same time.

His mother quietly trailed behind his antics, a little concerned, but not much. She reached down for her first taste of clover in a long time. The succulent fullness of the sweet clover was a dramatic change for her. For the sake of Sejanus and her other offspring, she had chosen an austere place to live. But this was summer. It seemed that no living creature could completely ignore the ripeness which could restore a badly depleted spirit so fully, so far in advance of yet another barren winter.

In summer the fat trout in the tiny brooks would leap simply for the sheer pleasure of it and then chase the lethargic, overfed chubs further and further down into the warm, undesirable holes far away from the cool, sheltering hemlock banks. The excessive forces which lay latent in the fat flanks of these wild trout was a common theme of nature in the summertime.

Indeed, the young of all carnivore and herbivore alike, would romp unrestrained when it was safe, giving back to their elders something far more substantial than ordinary instinct could prescribe. Even the mother of Sejanus, usually reticent to an extreme degree, even she was not immune to the pleasures of summer. In the dark warmness of the field, she let Sejanus slide further out ahead of her then she normally would.

She knew that he had alerted the other deer on the other side of the small block of woods with all his frolicking. She felt that there was no reason to be unduly alarmed by this. The rut was a long way off, and so far no matriarch had displayed a lot of hostility toward their presence in foreign territory. Still, she knew that Sejanus would soon spy them and might become alarmed by their nearness, so she moved closer to him to reassure him when the discovery of the other deer was made. She couldn't quite make them out yet, but Sejanus' mother could tell that there was more than one deer over there and that their ears were up. Sejanus soon had his ears up also. He heard his mother eating nearby and could tell by her body language that there was no cause for alarm. Fifty yards or so from him were two fawns with their mother, like his mother, not far behind.

Sejanus, being a single fawn, was somewhat longer and larger than the two youngsters in front of him. This would be the case throughout his life, for he was the exception rather than the rule. Still, the fawns in front of him carried themselves very well and were slightly wider in the front then was normal for their age.

When the youngsters realized that there was nothing to be afraid of, and that their mothers had, in effect, given them the green light to get to know each other, all hell broke loose. Sejanus ran toward the other two, jostled them a little, and soon all three of them were performing ungraceful caprioles as they tried to figure out how to play with each other.

This uncharacteristic abandonment of decorum and stealth provoked the same instinctive reaction in both the mothers. They lifted their noses into whatever prevailing breeze there was to see if anything other than themselves was afoot. Leaving each to scan what section of the field they could see the best, the two doe tested the shadows along the edge of the wide woods from front to back to make sure that the play in front of them was as safe as possible. This behavior was repeated every so often as they fed a bit and worked closer to each other so that their periodic surveillance would be tighter.

Once they felt that the situation was satisfactory, the two doe then regarded each other dispassionately. The mother of the twin fawns was a magnificent creature. No ordinary doe this, she was smaller and darker then the mother of Sejanus, but she was smaller and darker for a good reason. This was a deer bred for turning in tight quarters and blending in flawlessly with the subdued light of tangled brush. She was a swamp deer through and through. Not far from this field lay the biggest swamp around, and she was the undisputed queen of it.

She wasn't as long as the mother of Sejanus, but her front and rear ends were noticeably stocky and indicative of something grand and regal. Once sufficiently relaxed, she would glance at Sejanus from time to time as he fled by her. She had had a solitary fawn the year before and something about Sejanus reminded her of him.

She was qualified to recognize great potential, for this was the mother of Essene.

After a long while the fawns grew tired and all the deer lay down in the tall grass to let the faint breeze and gathering dew keep the bugs away. They slept before the mounting light of dawn prompted them to get up and stretch. It was time for them to part ways because they were from separate territories and it wouldn't do to form a bond unnecessarily.

Sejanus' mother urged him toward the corner of the woods that they had emerged from the night before. Sejanus sensed a certain unease in his mother so he complied without hesitation. Just as they reached the darkness of that corner, his mother glanced back at the mother of the two fawns. The unease that Sejanus felt emanating from his mother was actually an emotion that only the most intelligent of deer could fathom and, if only briefly, hold. As the mother of Sejanus gently urged him into the woods, she knew, in her heart, that she would never see this field again. Though not fully developed and comprehended, the mother of Sejanus was experiencing sorrow.

–CHAPTER 14–

So, thirty years prior to the birth of Sejanus, a period of intense logging caused the evaporation of a reliable mast crop in his home territory. This fact contributed heavily to the individual he became as an adult. There were still plenty of harsh ravines and extremely steep areas where, in good years, a mast crop could be found, but on the whole, Sejanus had to learn from a very early age how to get from point A to point B without getting devoured or otherwise slain.

There was no better teacher at how to accomplish this then his mother. For her, everything was cover and using cover to create optical illusions. A small fir or beech sapling with its fall leaves still intact, growing in the right place by a rock or slight depression in a side hill might be just enough to cause a hunter, just far enough away, to wonder, "Was that a squirrel or sneaking partridge there? Couldn't quite tell . . ."

By the time the hunter moved to a place where he could tell, Sejanus frequently would be as much as a quarter mile away. The secret was to always, every time, position yourself in a place where such deception could be so artfully practiced.

Getting yourself in a place where you presented a profile from either above or below was absolutely taboo in the world view of his mother. She was not easy to travel with, particularly in the fall when there was shin-fa about.

If she was going any distance at all, she would follow the ancient deer trails which had been established following the last ice age— only, however, if they met certain criteria. If there was too much open area on one side of a ridge compared to another side, Sejanus' mother would always choose the side with the most cover on it and never along the crest of said ridge.

Sejanus found it quite annoying and very tiring to travel along the sides of ridges instead of along their crests. After a few kicks and well placed bites however, he freely consented to following her lead and thereafter made this way of traveling a lifetime habit. It saved his life many times. When coming up from a gully or brook bottom, the drill was to aim for a mass of scrubby hemlock or fir just below the top of the hill one was climbing. If you got to this desirable cover safely, then you could ease yourself up to a position where you could take a gander around to determine whether or not to proceed to wherever it was you wanted to go. These were the procedures she drilled into him when they were making their way from place to place during quiet times. This was done in an attempt to avoid drawing attention to oneself. When true danger was evident however, all that quickly went out the window. The absolute terror when he realized that his mother was genuinely alarmed was almost suffocating. He always acted in a correct manner to that terror however, and was rewarded by another day of living.

His mother was more intelligent than most doe, but when the time of real danger arrived, only the genetic keys hidden inside the heart of Sejanus allowed him to pass the crash courses his mother threw at him as he strove to follow her during these dark moments.

Using any available bends and curves in the land, his mother would first attempt to gain some distance from that which was pursuing them. If necessary, top speed running and leaping through heavy brush or boulder fields, followed by sharp turns and super slow sneaking might be in order.

A couple of times, under great duress and strictly as a last resort, there would be the slight separation where his mother would try to lure off the threats while he, Sejanus, carrier of the genetic future, would use the lessons imparted to him to sneak off to what he deemed to be a respectable distance to await his mother's return.

Oh how black it was in those places. He learned the full measure of his young heart's courage at these times. Looking far downhill, as he was taught, a faint, almost imperceptible movement would always tempt him but he knew better; he waited. The movements would usually disappear as the great circles of his mother's supernatural ability to deceive reached their completion. Then, after the usual interminable period of waiting, there finally came a flick of ears nearby before their eyes made contact and then the ordeals were over.

This happened twice with coydogs and once with a bear. The episode with the bear was, by far, the most serious. Bears in the springtime are always very hungry and very persistent if they think a meal is imminent. Usually fawns are instructed to lie very still and let their lack of scent protect them from predators. The bear, which had flushed Sejanus from his bed, had experience in such matters. His mother had to apply every trick she had in her considerable arsenal to turn that bear around.

However, as bad as that bear had been, it was the shin-fa in the fall which concerned the mother of Sejanus the most. There wasn't much time, and it was an impossible goal, but if Sejanus' mother had her way, no shin-fa would ever lay their eyes on her son. And, though it was an impossible task, she nevertheless applied all her considerable talents to attempt to make that goal a reality.

–CHAPTER 15–

Earl's son, Johan, knew exactly where he was going. Fourteen going on forty when it came to trout fishing, Johan knew this was exactly the right time of the year to head to the deep, dark bend of Sadie's Brook. A week or ten days later then this would be too late. At that point the trout would have moved on further upstream to be closer to their fall spawning grounds. He had been told this, and now, after several years of actual experience, now he knew this to be a matter of unadulterated truth.

So, with a peach can full of fat, sassy worms that he had dug early that morning he hustled his way up through the first two fields before the heat of the day caused a thick bead of sweat to break out along his forehead. He tried not to hurry, but he had a thing about catching native brook trout.

Sadie's Brook was actually a small river if depth and width had anything to do with it.

The spot he was heading for was in very rough ground and therefore many of the trees along the brook's banks had not been cut. The trout loved it there, at least for a while. When the temperatures reached a certain height for a certain length of time and the apple blossoms began to stretch and open, then it was time to intercept the big, native brook trout on their way up above. Today they would be there—ten, twelve inches long, jet black with bright red spots circled with a vivid blue. No stocked trout here; these were the natives who had drifted back down into the deep spring holes in the alder swamp to winter out and survive another year.

Thinking of them drove Johan to hustle on through the end of the third field and onto a mossy remnant of an old logging road which would take him directly to the fishing holes he had in mind. Sweating profusely now, he paused momentarily to wipe his brow and cool off a little before setting out again in the quiet, mossy shade toward a corner in the road which was guarded by a thick stand of young hemlock.

After exiting the field that morning, Sejanus and his mother had wandered about somewhat aimlessly, admiring and partaking of what the level, fertile ground of that area offered them. Then, quite a ways off, they heard the sound of running water so they slowly fed their way in that direction. They hadn't drunk in a long time, and the hot day required more liquid refreshment then the lush vegetation was giving them.

Though the brook in front of them was guarded by a steep, substantial bank, it nevertheless didn't take Sejanus' mother very long to locate a small feeder brook which offered an easy way down to the deep, clean water of Sadie's Brook.

Once in the shade of a huge hemlock tree, she and Sejanus drank their fill; they began to look for an easier way back up the bank and retracing their steps up through the feeder brook. The brush along the feeder brook however, seeking the southwestern sun, was growing in the wrong direction and formed an effective barrier which discouraged them from ascending there. Just down from the feeder brook was a smooth section of the bank with some small hemlock at the top, which was just the type of cover that Sejanus' mother always aimed for when coming up out of a gully. Well, so much for infallible plans.

They used all the usual precautions coming

up the bank, but the breeze was consistently out of the south and therefore working against them. Perhaps that was why Sejanus' mother failed to detect anything until it was too late.

Johan, meanwhile, had been eagerly nearing the brook along the quiet, mossy road when the slightest of sounds off to his left, down over the bank, caught his attention. Other than his fishing pole, he didn't have anything to protect himself with. Gripped by a sudden, justifiable fear, he froze in his tracks. Then the largest, most magnificent doe he had ever seen more or less melted out of the brush not far from where he stood.

The doe sensed his presence almost immediately, and with a loud blat, she sailed across the road and out of sight. Keeping up with her with no apparent effort was the largest fawn that he would ever see.

Though it had been the intention of the mother of Sejanus never to allow Sejanus to be seen by a shin-fa, the inevitable failure to achieve this objective didn't bother her too much. After all, the shin-fa was an unknowable, omnipotent threat which was impossible for her kind to even begin to comprehend. They were a nuisance all the time, but their worst intrusions came in the fall when she and her kind were deeply involved with the business of procreation and therefore very vulnerable.

The only discernible weakness that she had ever seen in them was that they apparently had poor eyesight. When the shin-fa were ready to deliver their message of death, they would lift their great, dark, solitary horn and gaze through it to determine which unfortunate deer would meet its end.

The young shin-fa who had frightened her so badly at the road had been carrying a thin horn that she had never seen before. Why he had not elected to use it, Sejanus' mother did not know nor care. However, the incident had rattled her confidence for quite a while. But it was still summer so there was still plenty of time to learn from this mistake and to move on. It was important to her that she impart to Sejanus the unequivocal understanding that there was no end to the steps that made up the perpetual dance of avoidance.

–CHAPTER 16–

Originally, Sejanus' mother had intended to linger for an indefinite amount of time around that general area. However, after their encounter with the young shin-fa, she decided that it was best to move on. There were other feeding places that she wanted to show Sejanus, and, more importantly, several important game trails that he needed to see and eventually use as time went by.

After attending to such details, they traveled far enough and long enough to see that the beginning of the end of summer was at hand. There was no hurry, but his mother pointed her nose north and slowly headed for the hills which made up their home territory.

On their way back, they had a couple of episodes involving circumnavigating coydogs. These were glimpses more than anything and not really moments of fear or crisis. More than he could appreciate, his mother was encouraging him to sharpen his survival skills.

In fact, Sejanus had begun to notice that his mother was not discouraging small periods of exploring or separation on his part. Fall and then winter were approaching, and these would be periods of great uncertainty. His ability to exist independently of her had to be promoted as much as possible at this stage in his life. He needed to have enough rudimentary skills to carry on in her absence.

Her reaction to the coydog episodes was a good case in point. During the summer the coydogs had lots of things to feed on like voles or other rodents. If deer were foolish or careless, then they could still be on the menu, but on the whole, the coydog attitude was, "Why bother?"

The coydogs seemed to be content to let deer fatten up during the times of plenty so that the deer would provide them with even more nourishment during the cold, hard winter.

Sejanus' mother instinctively perceived this. So when she spied the telltale flickers of carnivorous movement heading their way, she immediately put Sejanus through a long, vigorous routine of evasive activity which served to reinforce the lessons she had taught him earlier that summer. He showed plenty of evidence that he had an exceptional genetic makeup when these incidents occurred. He was a very fast learner.

The whole summer sojourn had been done to give Sejanus every chance of surviving. He now knew where all the important game trails were. In the future, these would take him to where the main genetic gears of the white-tail world were turning or staying stagnant or rusty. If necessary, he now knew where to find other deer to be around when the safety of numbers came into play, as in the wintertime. She showed him the rivers, the brooks and hidden springs which defined what was available to him in terms of boundaries, protection and nourishment. In a relatively short period of time she had done it all and she had done it well. Even in the world of deer there are great differences between mothers, and the mother of Sejanus was one of the best.

It was when the leaves in the lowlands were just starting to turn color that she noticed a few beechnuts in the ravines leading up to their mountain home. In a vague, vexing sort of way this troubled and annoyed her. There weren't enough beechnuts to provide the deep layers of fat she would need to fight off the ravages of winter, but there were going to be enough to attract the attention of some of the deer from the surrounding lowlands. This, in turn, would be sure to trigger an increase in the number of shin-fa lurking in their territory when the fall came.

Usually the number of shin-fa, that far up into the hills during hunting season, was small due to the remoteness of the area and to the scarcity of deer. During this particular year the acorn crop had pretty much failed to materialize. The appearance of these few beechnuts meant that the probability that the remoteness of their home range would keep them safe was lowered. The equation had been changed and she knew it. She acted accordingly.

When the leaves fell and the sound of gunshots drifted up their way, she went to her favorite place to avoid predacious activity. At the end of a long flat of open, forty-year- old hardwood which sloped gently uphill, was a small knoll with a couple of mature white pine and some big hemlock on it. Just on the other side of this knoll was an old tote road, and just beyond the old tote road was a sunken area ringed by young hemlock. Not too far from this sunken area was the craggy, immense, rounded end of a steep mountain slope which could take her and

Sejanus great distances in a hurry if necessary. They had done the drill before, and if speedy evacuation was required, then the ancient, hemlock-covered tote roads which lead around and off this particular crag were well studied and known.

The family of Sejanus had used this area with good effect for generations. When the wind was from one direction, she and Sejanus would lay up on or around the pine knoll to watch the gradual slope below them. When the opposite was true, they went to the sunken area on the other side of the tote road to maintain their vigil there.

The hunting pressure that year increased until finally she and Sejanus would get up only at night or during periods of rain. It was an inconvenient but not impossible situation. By long experience the mother knew that the end of the hunting season was at hand. She had suppressed her urge to breed and could now see a time when that urge could be addressed and satisfied.

Then, one gray day, there came in a steady, light snow. She and Sejanus had wisely laid low while this was occurring so as not to leave any tracks about. The snow had a peaceful, lulling effect on her, and maybe she slept a bit. The shin-fa were upon them before she could react effectively. Then there was another sound just off to her right.

Blatting loudly as she rose, she then tore off to her left as she sought to attain the safety of the end of the pine knoll where she and Sejanus had frequently lay. From there she would decide how to begin making the first circle, which would lead the danger away from Sejanus.

Sejanus, seeing and hearing all this, promptly went the opposite way. He snuck down the hill for some distance until he reached the beginning of one of the hemlock-covered tote roads which led down off the mountain. There, as always before, he set up to await the return of his mother.

The suspense within him was stretched to its fullest tautness. Then, just when it seemed that that stretching could get no tighter, the long, black horn of the shin-fa unleashed its terrible thunder. Sejanus had never heard gunfire so close and it opened forever a horrible new window in him.

Never before that time had the trees seemed so high as they stretched in utter solitude above his isolated and lonely state. At that moment, in spite of everything that his mother had taught him, Sejanus then felt compelled to leave the safety of the sheltering hemlock to get himself to a place where he could see off a little. He heard the guttural sounds of the shin-fa communicating nearby. Another step and he was there. He was just in time to watch two of them stride purposefully away from him, leaving the blood of his mother on the freshly fallen snow as they dragged her body away.

–CHAPTER 17–

Unlike Sejanus, Essene had enjoyed the full benefits of having his mother nearby for the first, important year. Even Sejanus, in a roundabout way, even Sejanus could have credited his continued survival, if not directly to her, then at the very least to her immediate family. In truth, Sejanus never did see the mother of Essene again, but he did meet several of Essene's aunts and even an older sister of the future patriarch.

After his mother's death, Sejanus had drifted uncertainly down toward a region he figured would hold other deer. Mindful of the incident with the young shin-fa the summer before, he didn't go directly to that part of the forest where Essene's mother lived. He didn't have to. Once he got somewhat near that region, he ran into other deer and was, due to his immature status, allowed to hang around them at a respectful distance. He wasn't the first yearling to be orphaned, and a certain flexibility exists within the white-tail community for those of his type. He would be tolerated and that was enough.

While Essene had still been within the bosom of his mother's capable presence, he had been molded fully and completely into a creature of the swamp. Whereas a lot of deer knew of the swamp, traveled along its edges, and used it to escape from danger from time to time, Essene and his tribe actively embraced the swamp, and as much as possible, made it a part of themselves. In a very real way, thanks to his mother, when circumstances dictated, it seemed to those who were determined to harm Essene—it seemed to them that Essene was the swamp, a foggy, misty apparition.

And a large swamp it was. It stretched almost continuously between the bony, diminishing toes of two western foothills in Maine, foothills which eventually, after a hundred miles or so, eventually led up to the Presidential Mountains of New Hampshire.

Although interrupted occasionally by a few unsteady, inconsequential berms of pine and hemlock, the swamp ran between these two foothills for six or seven miles. Most of it was quite narrow, but in places the swamp bowed out to more than a mile across. Two distinct, narrow, deep brooks divided either end of the swamp as they bled into and out of two separate, boggy ponds. In and around these brooks and ponds were innumerable tiny brooks, springs and wet spots which sometimes showed water and sometimes didn't, depending on the season mostly. To the uninitiated, the tangled, wet mass presented a facade which bordered on the hostile.

Practically as soon as he was able to stand up, Essene's mother made it her business to make sure that Essene knew every square inch of it. Like Sejanus, Essene spent the first summer of his life on a long sojourn in and around the entire circumference of the majestic swamp.

His mother was an excellent guide and teacher. The first month of his life was spent going back and forth across a reasonably wide portion of the swamp's northern end. For the shin-fa at any rate, this was a formidable piece of real estate.

The brook which ran through here was a truly daunting barrier to the uninitiated. It was deceptively narrow, and in most places quite deep. For a hunter to step into its black, motionless water was to invite a miserable day trudging around with wet clothes—that's if the hunter could find a place that he thought he could leap across. The banks of the brook were almost uniformly crowded with ancient alders and shrubs which sprouted up out of dangerously unstable or outright muddy ground. There were places which were easily recognizable as deer crossings, but no self-respecting master buck would be caught dead using them except, of course, in the direst of emergencies.

Essene usually didn't have to worry on that account. In spaces too narrow to fit through, past walls of ancient alder too thick to leap between, Essene's mother, in this one important section of the swamp showed him a dozen places where he could use the friendly brook to keep himself well separated from any potential danger.

In the first month of his life, he was shown every safe path to every big white pine or white maple which signaled where the small, dry areas were in a thirty-five acre piece of swampland. That this strip of swampland was right where the two foothills, which hemmed in the swamp, started to reach up and gain the height and drainage necessary to reliably sustain a good mast crop was not noticed by many, but the ancestors of Essene had. Throughout his life, this section of the swamp would be Essene's core area.

Ironically, the best part of this particular swamp, besides its daunting, prohibitive size, was its close proximity to human beings. Where the foothills on either side tended to peter out, there happened to be several fields and apple orchards, which provided a much more dependable source of food then the fickle mast crops did. And, if one didn't care for those fields or orchards, then a cautious deer could wend themselves along ancient game trails to any number of alternate feeding areas.

Once his mother had finished giving Essene her grand tour of the swamp proper, she then set about giving him a crash course on the best ways to exit and enter what was to be his core area. After that, she then took the time to show him how to get to important places far beyond the swamp which would become increasingly more important to him as he grew older. A deer of his stature would need a lot of elbow room to achieve what nature had designed him for.

Though the swamp and its immediate environs was the proverbial land of plenty for deer in most regards, it nevertheless, in a paradoxical sort of way, had severe limitations. So much protective cover and abundant sources of food naturally made for a lot of deer, compared to where Sejanus and his tribe lived. Aside from the obvious problems of increased predatory activity and disease, the difficulty in achieving genetic improvement was much more pronounced here than one might think.

In a place where there were a lot of deer, there would also have to be a lot of bucks. Many of these animals were big, impressive specimens intent on leaving an appropriate mark on their race. Naturally the competition was fierce, with the emphasis being on brute strength and youth. Under these conditions, many otherwise worthy deer would meet their early demise. The status quo seemed to require a lot of dying.

The rashness of youthful enthusiasm was one of the biggest reasons that the shin-fa were so successful in killing big bucks, especially young, big bucks. No buck could afford to wait. Even Essene, during his early eruptions of breeding activity, even Essene initially took chances which easily could have gotten him killed. But luck and the swamp were on his side.

It didn't take him too many years to adopt a healthy paranoia when it came to chasing doe in heat. As he approached true maturity, he would only emerge from his lair in the swamp at night, preferably during moonless nights. This helped him to avoid not only shin-fa and coydogs, but other big bucks as well, and that was important.

Of all the dangers he faced in the fall, fighting other big bucks was a danger he diligently tried to avoid. He did it only when he absolutely had to. He actually, due to his relatively high intelligence, would take steps to avoid confrontation whenever possible. Fighting took a huge toll out of a deer. Obviously, the threat of serious injury or even outright death was always a possibility when two massive bucks crossed paths. However, even if injury was· avoided, the stripping away of vital, core energy in the face of an approaching winter was the main danger of fighting too much. The depleting effect of prolonged conflict definitely is a leading cause of death in dominant bucks. Over time, Essene developed a strategy for lessening his exposure to unnecessary overexertion.

Around his core area in the swamp, when the time came to rub the velvet from his massive antlers, he would take the time to find a large basswood or poplar tree near an open place. Most bucks rub a lot of trees when the rut is upon them, but not Essene. He didn't like to advertise his presence any more then he had to. A few well-placed rubs over a large region told all who understood what was going on. He placed a couple of these rubs near his core area as a fair warning. Any bucks encroaching on the doe of that region were in danger of losing their life if they weren't worthy.

More and more, however, as he was reaching the prime of his life, Essene began to rely less on the number of doe he bred and more on the quality of the doe he mated with. Around his core area, early in the season, he would mate with quite a few doe but then, very quickly, he would shift gears and become very secretive and nocturnal.

For Essene, the progression went from late, later, and then, finally, latest. As the years went by he went from seeking does that came into heat late, then to does that were even later, until finally, at the very height of his prime, he would, after the initial burst of energy around his core area, seek out only those does who, by genetic design, held out until the very end of the rut before they allowed a buck to approach them. This behavior tended to keep him relatively fresh and in one piece. It also cemented his place in the future hierarchy of the white-tail race.

–CHAPTER 18–

Phyla was the matriarch of a small but influential group of deer. This group lived in a place which, for some reason, seemed to be important, not only to the local white-tail world but to the larger white-tail universe as well.

To the casual observer this would all be a matter of pure, random luck, and on the surface, the casual observer would be right. But at some point over hundreds, or thousands, of years, luck stops being luck and evolves into something else. A repetition of a set of circumstances over a certain period of time elevates a condition into a state of unshakable knowledge.

The world of the white-tail has many places where the invisible gears which drive the dynamics of their social workings collide or mesh together. By luck or by design the territory which Phyla presided over was a place where a lot of bigger and smaller white-tail gears met. She was the oil which lubricated this very important junction.

Here the flat lands of New England met the mountains of western Maine and New Hampshire. From here the genetic stew would work its way up into northern and eastern Maine and then finally spill out across the St. John River to the rest of the white-tail domain. Phyla, at this point in time, was the tip of the flame which boiled the blood and moved the stew.

On the whole, deer behavior doesn't really seem to vary that much, but again, time gives everything the necessary twists that will unwind into the designs of nature. A slight accentuating, promoting a certain amount of leverage over a certain amount of time had produced a perfectly predictable, Darwinian result; Phyla was one of the most intelligent deer alive.

Of course with great gifts came great responsibilities and dangers. What she had to give had to be given to the best, and only the best. She had been supplied the tools to accomplish a great task by generations of deer who fluctuated between being highly intelligent and dangerously paranoid. If the paranoia part of the equation became too pronounced, then the herd would suffer. Breeding would become spotty and disease would increase. Luckily for the white-tail tribe, Phyla's paranoia was well tempered by intelligence and courage.

As taught to her by her mother and grandmother, Phyla adopted a simple, effective behavior to get her genes to the top shelf. Every year, toward the end of summer it was the same old drill. Phyla, along with her immediate family and maybe a cousin or two, would break away from the main hub of summer deer activity and head toward a generalized spot which had been "given" to her by her mother.

This spot was near a large field which was generously surrounded by an expansive area of thick, young hemlock and fir. It was important that she could hide as long as possible during the rut. When the rut took off in earnest late in October, the generalized spot which they had been hanging out in for the last two months became a much more specific spot. This specific spot had water nearby and was located near an ancient, important game trail. At this point the entourage accompanying Phyla would spring into action, or more appropriately, fail to spring into action. That is to say, being of the same genetic inclination as Phyla was, they all came into heat late.

The young or otherwise inferior bucks, driven out by the better bucks around the main deer hub some distance off, would come sniffing around first, only to be driven off by the pinned back ears and slashing hooves of dominant female deer not ready to breed.

But, as that situation changed, as one by one the members of Phyla's harem bowed to the urges of nature according to their age and status, Phyla would soon find herself forced to keep as isolated from them as she possibly could. She, being the matriarch, would have to be the last doe to come into heat. With her little herd of compatriots going back and forth all over the place leaving scent and sign everywhere, Phyla would retire to her final "spot." At this special, hidden place she could await what she expected to be a superior buck once she could no longer restrain the urges of nature. Of course, this really wasn't any secret. Every self-respecting buck for miles around knew all about this little charade of Phyla's. But few, if any, ever dared to press home their desire for her. Many otherwise brave and worthy bucks would head in her direction with the best of intentions, only to be plunged headlong into a world of deep darkness caused by the brilliant presence of one of Essene's fresh, bright rubs on a huge cedar tree not far from Phyla's special spot.

–CHAPTER 19–

In an unusually fertile and abundant vale early that fall, a matriarch coydog devoured the last available vole. Unwilling to believe that the easy living was at an end, she and her pack milled around for a while before it became apparent to them that the fullness of the fields thereabouts was now empty. Still, reluctant to leave a place of plenty, the matriarch rested in the sun for as long as she could before the clan began to pester her to set the gears of necessity into motion once more. Growling once in frustration, she finally led her pack out toward a different area where some other feed could be found.

They had not gone far before they spooked a family of foxes who carefully fled before the superior predators. Sliding away in the opposite direction that the coydogs were traveling, the foxes managed to flush the covey of partridges that they had been stalking before the coydogs had barged in.

The partridge, long aware that something had been lurking behind them, took off with an unusually loud burst of energy which had been slowly building up while they waited for the cause of that lurking to reveal itself. Using that built-µp energy to the utmost, the partridge quickly reached the crest of a steep slope, which overlooked the black ribbon of a silent, hidden brook. Using the slight up drafts emanating from the sunny slope and the cool, dark brook, the birds silently glided much further then they normally would have, coming finally to rest in some thick fir, far to the other side of the brook.

While doing this they had flown over an old raccoon that had been busy foraging in the dark interior of the brook's embrace. Recognizing the fact that gliding partridges were probably a bad thing for him, the raccoon wisely decided that it was time to head for greener pastures. While thus alertly deviating his path away from the approaching danger, the old raccoon managed to prod a reluctant flock of turkeys to turn more to their left than they had wanted to.

One of them broke into a quick trot and the rest followed suit. The glint and flash of their silent running through the dappled sunlight of the thick forest roiled up a bunch of resting songbirds. Their scattering apprehension in turn ignited a large flock of restless crows whose raucous calling lifted ears and nostrils for miles around.

The success of the voles in the fertile vale had attracted the coydogs, the cause of their destruction. All the unwitting abundance had planted the many seeds which would destroy the balance which had supported that abundance. The lowering sun, the lessening light, the bright fall foliage, compressed the minute springs which were to propel the blood through the blank whiteness of perpetual winter. The void created by the apparent destruction of the voles would set the stage for the life-giving vacuum, which would draw in all the agents that would set up the next round of fulfillment and plenty.

No good machine can lie idle for long without the vital components and seals cracking or otherwise breaking down. The gears of the machine must turn to lift the oil, the lifeblood of the machine, onto the bearings which support the stress of work and moving. After all, machines are nothing more than an abstract reflection of the inner body of their creators, built to achieve the permanence of endless repetition.

Nature likewise has her gears and her means of motivation.

After the crows had ceased their harsh rhetoric, a pair of opportunistic blue jays set out to investigate the land in that direction to see if any food could be had there. This resulted in a group of chickadees, seeking to avoid the aggressive, dangerous jays, to alter their course and to filter into the protective, young hemlock which grew in abundance at the edge of a big swamp.

Feeding on the tips of the hemlock as they made their way fretfully along, the chickadees soon made their way deeply into the wetland. Bobbing, weaving, flitting along, they eventually made their way over a large deer who watched their arrival with keen interest. Random, irrelevant, inconclusive messages were constantly coming to him along the forest's imperfect lines of communication. However, as the chickadees approached and then went over him, they created a series of black spots when they got between him and the sun. He connected the dots between the spots, like a sort of Morse code, and the seeds of doubt were planted. Nature's gears were moving, and the message the chickadees delivered was as important as it was clear; this huge area needed more and smarter deer.

–CHAPTER 20–

No matter how fierce the raging storm, no matter how deep the surging tide gathers and floods up into the tidal streams, no matter how long the irresistible force has its way with the immovable object, there always comes a time when the tide wearily covers the last pebble before it retreats back into the infinite sea.

At the end of his sixth summer, Essene felt the tide within him quiver at the brink of its fullness. There was no alarm in him as he felt the beginnings of his autumn self-start to emerge from the chrysalis of his placid summer being. Lying in the morning sun, the maple leaves just starting to turn red high above him, Essene watched the bugs dancing in a pool formed by the previous night's rain as he rested in his swampy lair. Listening to the pleasant gurgle of the brook behind him, Essene felt no trepidation about the coming breeding season. Any diminishing power, even if he was able or willing to detect it, was not now.

His mighty antlers, arched high over his face in the classic way of all swamp bucks, had nothing in them which suggested weakness or retreat. His thick neck, not yet swollen with the rut, was still twice the size of most of the rival bucks in this region, and it was still unscarred for no deer had ever seriously challenged him and escaped uninjured. Yes, for most of the year Essene was a gentle giant, content to watch the frolicking of fawns as he fattened up in the secret high meadows of his summers. But now, with the turning of every scarlet leaf by the infantile, autumn breezes, now he could feel the thin red waves of his blood rising as it began to take away the playfulness in his eyes.

Something was amiss. He sensed that his power was still intact and even at its full height, but like the shadow of the tattletale blue jay, a wave of trepidation passed over him and almost caused him to get up. He stayed in his place of rest. Whatever was coming was not here yet.

But the tide of his fullness was not permanent; this he sensed. A deep current of urgency he had never experienced before momentarily unsettled and confused him. He waited. Always in the past, his moments of unease and fear had eventually worked for him and guided him to make proper responses to proper circumstances. The time for concern was not now. He had no way of knowing exactly when that concern would evolve into a need for specific action.

But he did have a pretty good idea where that need for specific action would have to be applied. The blue jay who had just passed over him was jabbering in the background, annoying Essene more than it should have. Weren't they, the jays, always waiting and hoping for his kind to die? Was not feasting on each individual deer's destruction in the fall an integral part of each individual blue jay's main goal in life? Weren't they, the jays, always threatening to give away the white-tails' most secret hiding spots to the dreaded shin-fa?

Of course, being the gluttonous morons that they were, they would frequently, though inadvertently, help the deer from time to time. Becoming excited whenever a shin-fa passed nearby, the jays would lose all sense of decorum and squawk loudly in hopes of guiding a hunter toward the nearby prey.

But that time was not now. The sun was far too high in the early autumn sky for the jabbering jay in the background to mean much of anything. Soon enough however the sun's zenith would sink lower and lower against the nearby western mountains. The winds would become frequently cold and out of the north. Then the calls of the jays would take on their full, sinister resonance as the diminishing light revealed the full extent of the danger that the deer found themselves in. Though always demoralizing, the noisy jay behind Essene seemed to be promising that an even tighter octave would be enlisted to help the shin-fa this year.

And it wasn't just the cold which would come easing out of the north this year. The jay in the background told Essene about this also. Gloating, arrogant, enthusiastic in his unpleasant proclamations, the jay, in his obscure, roundabout way, was glad to inform Essene that the die had been cast and that a certain grim destiny would have to be confronted. At that time, in this year, and in this year only, a threat would wend its way alongside the first cold winds of winter, though, of course, Essene had no real way of knowing exactly what kind of a threat would appear. But, that being as it may, he nevertheless had a pretty good idea where a need for some sort of action against that threat would probably have to be applied. Without realizing it, Essene found himself looking up towards the area where Phyla would someday soon be waiting for him.

–CHAPTER 21–

Phyla herself was experiencing some of the same forebodings that Essene was. At this time she was still in her summer range, but on its outer edge. To her it seemed as though she had been living on some sort of an edge all summer. Was it more rain, more thunder, more sun cutting through the unsettled weather? Were there more young partridge, more baby rabbits, more callous crows deliberately belittling or somehow interfering with every decision she made? Even when everything was utterly devoid of wind, everything quiet and deadly still, even then Phyla could still feel a great, dark current tugging at her, pulling her early and unhappily away from her summer pleasantries.

But there was more to it than the obvious, more to it than the usual inexplicable evolutions of weather cycles and a natural change in birth rates. Like Essene, Phyla's power of reproduction was nearing the time when that ability would begin to ebb. But also like Essene, she instinctively knew that her ability to reproduce at a high level was intact for now. In fact, she correctly surmised that her power to reproduce was never greater and never needed as much as it was needed right now, this year.

Sometimes this kind of tension will wear down a lesser or ordinary doe and cause them to come into heat earlier than usual or to cease coming into heat at all, to go barren. But Phyla was no ordinary doe.

Though the undeniable presence of an extraordinary tension was forcing her to leave the orbit of her summer activities early, she would not, under any circumstance, allow external forces to dictate the turning of her internal timetables. Somehow she knew that it was very important not to fall into an early estrus. Perhaps she was hoping that leaving the central hub of white-tail activity and that the extra elbow room she would thereby achieve would help to take the "heat" off. All of the feelings that she was vaguely experiencing were incorporated into a plan of action while the rest of the local white-tail herd was blithely eating clover under a hot, summer sun.

But the innermost, invisible core of all the white-tail gears was violently quivering in anticipation of a coming change. Nothing is more permanent then the absolute coupling of certainty with uncertainty. When you peel back an onion you reach a point when there is nothing there, yet the onion grows. The peeling back of the layers of the white-tail onion threatened to leave nothing, but Phyla was made of the right stuff to resist this illusion. She and her entourage slowly headed north.

Happily, this diversion seemed to help ease the tension for a while. They meandered around quite contentedly for rather an extended period of time before the pressure emanating from the pent up gears of the white-tail world would encourage them to move forward to the place of reckoning. By the time the first sounds of the shin-fa entering the woods to hunt came to them, Phyla and her group were already near the place of her secret waiting.

It was a long month for Phyla. For whatever reason, more and bigger bucks then usual came earlier and left later, depending on which of her entourage came into heat. After all, they had their place of importance within the white-tail hierarchy, and they seemed to be more intent than ever to secure their place within that hierarchy. Phyla found all this extremely aggravating. Still she persevered and waited.

The gears were almost invisible now as they stretched up through the cold November nights to mesh with the unknowable, mysterious fluids of creation. She headed to the darkest, most secret place she could think of while sending her little group scattering amongst the surrounding brush to give her a bit more time. Soon would be the moment of her greatest danger. When she came into heat, she would have to mate with the first superior buck that happened to come her way. She was way too important, genetically speaking. For her to attempt to deny a big buck his way could well prove fatal.

–CHAPTER 22–

Earl sat on the edge of his bed, looking at the darkness outside his window. This was the last day and he was glad. Work had kept him out of the woods for most of the season, but when he had hunted he had hunted hard. This sort of intense hunting had led to a type of chronic fatigue that he didn't need.

His usual hunting partner would not be with him today; that would determine how he would hunt once he got underway. It was cold out so he decided that he would still hunt during the morning up along the garden field area and then spend the rest of the day sitting at his usual place.

His enthusiasm for this prospect wasn't anywhere near as high as it had been two years earlier. Sitting for dozens of hours at the same place and never seeing anything was not a conducive factor in developing the good, steely resolve that was necessary to defeat the fidgeting which was sure to guarantee even a young, inexperienced buck a long, happy life.

Taking naps wouldn't help either. The colossal boredom that would develop when confronted with the absolute certainty that there wasn't a deer within several miles of where you were sitting could only be appeased by allowing the head to go down and letting the eyelids drop peacefully over blurry eyes. This was always supposed to happen for only a few seconds. However, too frequently harmless naps turned into bouts of snoring, which would eventually wake a hunter up after many long, crucial minutes of sleeping had gone by.

The waking up was bad also. The sudden, dangerous jolt of regaining consciousness would always be followed by a great flood of guilt and a recognition of the sure, absolute fact that the biggest deer in the territory must have crossed the trail while one was engaged in such a peaceful slumber. These episodes would scar the hunter's psyche and work to drain his resolve when approaching his sitting place in future years.

As Earl pulled on his long johns, he made up his mind that no scarring would occur today. This day he would pay strict attention right to the last light. That being decided he pulled on his slippers and got ready to head downstairs to make the coffee. He leaned over on the way out of the bedroom and patted his wife's butt. "See ya this evenin'," he whispered. His wife managed a groan of resentment by way of response.

For a time Sejanus had felt himself to be adrift. As the rut had progressed and deepened, he had wandered around the extreme outside limits of Essene's territory and had bred in a random, opportunistic manner. Though the temptation to mate with a greater number of does was great, he nevertheless managed to be discreet. Celibacy had no place in the makeup of a buck of Sejanus' stature, but he did manage to stay out of the main hub of that particular white-tail community. Something told him that his main objective lay somewhere along the outside edge of the territory.

However, hanging around the outer limits of Essene's domain, breeding indiscriminately, didn't exactly endear him with the leading bucks of the adjacent territories. One buck in particular took great umbrage at the haphazard manner with which Sejanus was conducting himself while he was deciding what to do in Essene's home range.

This fellow had coupled great brawn with

great courage to carve out for himself a significant chunk of white-tail territory. But he didn't have the complete package which was needed to challenge a master buck. His intelligence didn't anywhere near match his courage and brawn.

If he had been anywhere near smart enough, he would have taken one look at Sejanus and realized that he was, after all, perhaps a couple of years past his prime. And besides that, if he had been smarter, this buck would have realized that that old ligament problem in his left hind leg never did heal up the way he hoped it would. But he was strong and he was brave and he was angry and the challenge was laid down.

The minute their great horns were entangled, Sejanus was able to decipher the messages of the weaknesses contained in his challenger's movements. The challenger, for his part, soon recognized the inescapable fact that he might very well have voluntarily joined horns with his own executioner. Still, the fight was not brief. After plowing up a considerable piece of forest land, the challenger slipped going over a rock and took advantage of a brief separation to turn tail and run.

At such times in the past, Sejanus had pursued such pretenders and had inflicted great humiliation and punishment on them when their guard was down. But for now, enraged though he was, for now Sejanus was simply relieved to be rid of the challenger's great horns.

Anytime he locked horns with a rival buck, there was always the distinct possibility that the horns might not unlock. Sejanus was intelligent enough to sense this, and after all, this battle had been a reflex action more than anything else. The momentary exhilaration of this meaningless victory quickly gave way to a state of exhaustion when he realized how impotent he felt as he stood at the edge of Essene's home turf.

The hour of the rut was getting late, and he still had no indication as to the real direction he must soon take. A lesser buck might have panicked and started thrashing about wildly in an attempt to forcefully promote his meeting with destiny. Somehow Sejanus found it within himself not to give way to what would have amounted to a surrender to terror.

He waited. He found a dry, hemlock knoll overlooking a dark ravine and he waited for two days. He could feel the pressures of the great gears of the white-tail universe starting to turn, and he had to be on the right side of them when the fateful moment of hidden movement occurred. If he sensed that he was on the wrong side of the meshing, then he would have to attempt to slip through to the other side before being crushed and cast off into genetic oblivion.

Most bucks would flee from this moment, for the gears were slippery and the footing treacherous. Sejanus, with an effortless extension of his spirit, didn't even begin to hesitate as he flowed through the impending disaster. Instantly, one of the truly original game trails, literally almost as old as the hills, presented itself like a neon sign, and right smack-dab in the middle of this brand new day, right in plain view of everyone, he was on his way to Phyla.

Earl had had good intentions. He had put on extra clothes and had stuffed some extra trail mix into the unessential pockets of his heavy hunting coat to sustain himself through the long, cold difficult hours that he had envisioned enduring on the stand. But it didn't quite pan out that way.

It was very cold, the coldest day of the year, and as he trudged along, it occurred to Earl that he wasn't young anymore. Remembering the boredom and the uselessness of all the past expenditures of what was now appearing to be the precious, remaining hours of his life, Earl found it ridiculously easy to find ample reasons to avoid his sitting area.

As the crisp sun found the tips of the tallest hemlocks, a ragged, naked chant escaping from a hungry flock of crows was greeted by a nearby gunshot. Earl had already left the garden field and was carefully slipping up an old tote road when he heard the shot. He instantly eased down toward the direction that he felt the shot had come from.

When in trouble, he knew where deer tended to cross Sadie's Brook. These things happened. He felt an unsubstantiated surge of completely false optimism that if he got to the right place at the right time, that the hunt could well be over. If correct, he would soon be home with venison in the pot and another great hunting story to burden his wife with.

He thought of his wife and smiled. She had no idea why he tormented the deer the way he did. It, deer hunting, seemed to arouse in her husband a certain enthusiasm which she had never felt inclined to discourage. After a successful deer hunt he could be very sweet. Were not the November nights dark enough without being a complete imbecile? When the hunter came home from the hills, give him the blazing hearth and the soft rug on the floor if he so desired. It all seemed to work very well over the years.

Anyway, a shot at what was probably a coydog took Earl very easily away from his intended goal of sitting all day without moving a muscle. He hung around the brook crossing far longer than he should have until he let guilt drag him meekly by the nose up beyond the garden field to the sitting area that his grandfather had told him about so many years ago.

As he got his fluffy plastic seat out onto an old oak stump which was nestled up against a young rock maple tree, Earl was struck once again with the ubiquitous obscurity of the place he had chosen to spend so much time sitting at. When he had first started hunting here, he was convinced that this was the "ancient game trail" that his grandfather had spoken of.

His initial optimism was well seasoned now. He had never seen a deer here. But this was the last day of this season and he was glad. The sun was starting to creep halfway up the tallest pines when he ate the last bits of his crumbled trail mix. Once he finished doing that, he settled in and resolved to spend the last few hours of the season in a state of complete motionlessness. After all, he figured , he owed it to the day, and to the memory of his grandfather.

For a while all went well. He had dressed warmly in the morning, and as the sun raced rapidly up the tall pines and prepared to slide down behind the mountains in back of him, Earl took the usual solace in the fact that the day would soon be over and that then he could return home to select the rug of his choosing.

However, as always, when the sun reached the very tops of the trees, the whole process slowed way down. Suspended in the suddenly, rapidly increasing cold, Earl found himself at the place where it was evident that the day was never going to end.

The sun stopped moving, and the old, old questions carefully reared their persistent heads out of the reluctant shadows which emerged from a sun that apparently had no real intention of ever setting. The grim, certain despair of enduring another year of failing to get a deer was soon replaced with the more pertinent questions of mortality and the overbearing need to accept one's humble position in the overall scheme of things.

Without being fully aware of it, Earl soon assumed the attitude and outlook of the desperate sailor clinging to the mast of a destroyed sailing ship as it floated on the desolate bounty main. No land in sight, only the endless ocean before and after. Earl could only endure and hope that the faith given to him by his doubting ancestors would be enough to ease him forward to the next bleak horizon and a possible rescue.

When the sun finally evaporated from the top of the last tall pine, and he could truly begin to allow himself to think of an honorable retreat to home and hearth—at that very moment of surrender, Earl saw something, and in the way of all hunters, thought, *Wait . . . wait a minute . . . wait . . . .*

–CHAPTER 23–

Essene had ignored all the protocol which had heretofore   guided his life. He had never felt such pressure as he was now under. It was very painful, but he was not afraid, only concerned with the task at hand.

At this time of the year he had always made it a point to become a nocturnal creature. If he were unlucky, this habit wouldn't save him from the coydogs for they hunted at night also. But he didn't care about them particularly. It was the shin-fa which poised the greater threat, and he had always treated this threat with the respect that it deserved. So he had done his breeding at night and had then returned to his core area in the swamp during the day to rest until the next evening.

Suddenly, out of the blue, an impulse came to him that only a deer of his stature could comprehend. He had to stay closer to the place where he knew Phyla would soon be in heat. The peak of his life force would soon be matched with that of Phyla's if he were brave enough, strong enough, and lucky enough to mate with her in this particular year. They had mated before but this, he strongly felt, this was the one that mattered.

So, in a dense fir thicket set amongst even denser fir thickets, Essene laid down in a graying dawn to hopefully wait out the day in somewhat unfamiliar territory. She was up ahead there somewhere, and, hopefully, he would go to find her in heat that night. However, if circumstances dictated, he would take her in broad daylight if he had to. He had never stood by decorum in the past and he had no intentions of starting to do so now.

He tried to rest that day but sleep wouldn't come. Slowly, as the noonday passed and the shadows of the afternoon grew long, slowly a great rage began to secure possession of him, for he perceived, without a shadow of a doubt, that Phyla wasn't the only deer up ahead of him that mattered. With quivering disbelief he realized that a great challenger was nearby and would soon have to be dealt with.

He waited as long as he could stand it. Then,

just as the sun was about to set, he got himself up and prepared to leave the protective embrace of the heavy fir grove. It was still far too light for him to feel very comfortable about moving out in the open, but at the same time, he nevertheless realized it was far too late to worry about that. The die had been cast, and he had to get to his destination before those dice had settled long on the proverbial table.

The air was motionless. As he neared the edge of the fir thicket, Essene lowered his nose to the ground to seek out information about what lay before him, but nothing was forthcoming.

Essene dawdled for a few moments alongside the last protective branches of the last fir thicket. There was no smell, no sound, and no sight of anything which indicated danger. What was he to do?

He collected himself for a few moments more and then he made a decision. Then, just as he had succeeded in gathering up his courage to emerge from the fir, there came a sudden, vile squawking of blue jays from the hill above him. Ordinarily, this would have given him pause, but with a formidable challenger nearby, the treacherous screams of the jays only managed to goad him forward at a faster pace than he really wanted to go. He had to see what had caused the jays to call out, as soon as possible. Without further ado he headed up the hill.

Essene had a good idea where Phyla would be. After proceeding through some heavy cover for a quarter of a mile, he soon saw the obscure beginning of the game trail that he was looking for. Right at the edge of the game trail was a young, bushy hemlock tree that he decided to hide behind until it got just a little bit darker. He could smell Phyla from where he was.

Then, two hundred yards in front of him, behind other thick cover, Essene saw a quick flicker of movement. He knew instantly what it was. It was Sejanus, who had seen Essene at exactly the same moment.

The setting late November sun had been bathing the frigid air in a soft, pinkish light but no longer was this the case for Essene. The low, bitter rage which had been building up in him all that day suddenly erupted until everything he saw was viewed through the blood-red lens of a savage anger which knew neither boundary nor reason. Essene took a few steps forward to issue his challenge, and then, right as he and Sejanus' eyes locked once more through the tangled brush, right at that very moment Essene was swiftly unsheathed from reality.

A few miles from where Essene's inert body now lay, a placid river had been winding its way calmly through the beginning of the swamp which had served as Essene's home. Almost immediately after the sound of the shot which had taken his life had faded off into the surrounding mountains, a sudden ripple appeared over the surface of the water. The water, too late, reached out to slow down that which was passing. The remaining leaves of autumn turned as though facing a storm and joined the birds and the fish in a futile attempt to secure that which could not be secured. Essene's spirit, as brave in death as it had been in life, knew where it deserved to be. With one final, gigantic leap, his spirit cleared the blue of earth and found its rightful place amongst the dark, starry river of eternity.

–CHAPTER 24–

Immediately after the tragedy, Sejanus, rightfully so, perceived himself to be in great danger. After all, there very well could have been more than one shin-fa lurking nearby.

Resisting the urge to turn and flee like a yearling, Sejanus instead lowered his head slightly and froze. He then smelt very carefully the currents of air running along the forest floor. There was movement far out in front of him heading toward the body of Essene. Correctly, Sejanus perceived that he had not been spotted, and that this movement poised no danger to him.

He took a slow, single step backward, and then another, keeping his head low as he did so. After testing the air thoroughly, he repeated this procedure a couple of times. Until now, the cover around him had been full and good. However, once that cover of young pine and hemlock began to thin out into a stand of small beech whose leaves were still attached, Sejanus knew he had to change tactics. Gingerly, softly yet with an amazing swiftness, he turned around and got down on his belly.

The stand of young beech now facing him had a series of extremely small hummocks and almost imperceptible gullies running for about a hundred yards until the beech stand ran into another bunch of young pine and fir. Taking ample time to test the wind before each move, he slowly made his way on his belly toward the dark softwood growth in front of him. Any noise or suggestion of movement prompted him to cease his crawling and lower his head until he could decide whether or not any of these noises or movements constituted a real danger. Once he got into the fir and pine, he slowly regained his feet and then snuck along a distance which he felt would place himself outside the orbit of any immediate threat. Once he felt safe enough, Sejanus was content to wait for the ugly sounds of the triumphant shin-fa to die down and then fade away. Only when it was completely dark did he get up to search for Phyla.

Other than the clucking of a couple of opportunistic ravens who had wasted no time finding and feasting on Essene's mortal remains, the forest was now bathed in a silence which perfectly matched the nearly complete darkness of a new moon. Still, the stars shone, and that light was sufficient for Sejanus to move forward.

At first the search was daunting, for Sejanus was on unfamiliar ground, and he could only rely on his inner compass to guide his steps. He came back out to the game trail just below the spot where the shin-fa had ambushed Essene. Its hateful smell still lingered in the air, along with the strange, chemical odor of the gunpowder which had been incidentally scattered about the area when the lead bullet had left the gun's barrel. He turned to the right and followed the trail up the hill. He didn't go far when, to his left, he noticed dark movements within the darker shadows of the surrounding forest. As if by design, a couple of Phyla's entourage had pressed toward Sejanus to gain his attention. He knew what this meant. With a great surge of anticipation he abandoned all caution, cut through the presence of the two doe that had come out to meet him, and then he headed in a straight line directly up to Phyla's secret place.

She was easy to find then. Once he got to within fifty yards of her, Sejanus had no trouble whatsoever spotting the whites of her eyes as they anxiously awaited to behold the most important buck she would ever mate with. Instantly, all the springs of her biological clock unwound at a feverish pace as every pore of her feminine being erupted in an unrestrained joy.

Sejanus' mother would have been proud of him. Just like his magnificent father, Sejanus lowered his tremendous antlers, ripped apart some otherwise heathy young fir saplings and announced his intentions with no ambiguity whatsoever.

Usually under these circumstances, Phyla would have led her would-be suitor on a small jaunt around the countryside just to make sure that she wasn't about to allow herself to mate with a leper. This time, however, she just got herself clear of the dense thicket she had been hiding in so that neither she nor Sejanus would get hurt by the brush.

If the truth be told, there was no need of any further sexual activity once the initial meeting had been consummated. But the forest was full of brutes, and Sejanus was in no hurry to leave her.

They didn't exactly work on their suntans or anything, but something resembling a vacation occurred while Sejanus tended to her and protected her from being harassed or bullied by any big buck that happened to be in the immediate vicinity. Any would-be pretender to the throne would have to pass through him if they were going to dislodge the fetus now growing within her. That wasn't going to happen.

Sejanus stayed with her until Phyla's heat abated and then ceased altogether. Winter was now fast approaching, and he knew that she was the last doe he would have that year. It was time to return to an area near his craggy home where he knew how to get the necessary things to survive the lean times ahead. Traveling at night, he slowly meandered toward the place of his birth. Two weeks after he had left Phyla, right after the first serious snowfall of the year, he rounded the crest of a ledge and stood there gazing at the distant mountains of his home range. Overhead, the distant galaxies ground their way along, lighting the way for him now, and forever. Those great gears which had forced his actions, outwardly mindless, gave forth a beautiful music as they beheld Sejanus standing on that barren ledge, content to live out his life in this world before contributing his essence to their joyous sound. There was absolutely no worry about his place either in this world or the next because he was, after all, a *master buck*.

About the Author

Andrew R. Bennett has lived his entire life in the mountains of western Maine. At a very early age, during the extremely harsh winters of the 1960s, he developed a deep love and respect for the white-tail deer and their ability to survive.

Mr. Bennett graduated in 1976 from the University of Southern Maine with a Bachelor of Science degree. This is his second novel, and most of it was conceived while he was deer hunting.